The Beginners Book of Ogam Tree Healing

'I am breath'

Other Books by Thomas Marty

Thomas Marty has also written two books of fantasy short stories:

The Way of the World available on Amazon, lulu and kindle. This debut book for Thomas Marty comprises 15 short fantasy stories, mainly inspired by the city of Cambridge and beyond. Meet an eclectic bunch of characters: the Crowman of Jesus Green - a new slightly suspect superhero for the 21st Century; Amy, who has an alarming brush with fate when truth pays her a visit; the fantastical reincarnation of the Bansurist of Bewindhi in the heart of King's College Chapel; the evil presence lurking inside a derelict house in Sturton Street and the postman who delivers more than he should. To name but a few.

a little of what you fancy, available on Amazon, lulu and kindle. In this second collection of fantasy stories, meet... the floored genius locked in a fight with his nemesis, who then realises he needs her help to promote his new invention... the modern day Pilgrim investigating his spirituality whilst struggling to read the train schedule... the survivors dealing with devastating earth changes... Dave Green who buys into the idyllic rural dream only to discover the truth is more alarming... Geoffrey and his invisible friend, who together fight against his abusive nanny and the stigma of being unwanted... the Bull God Mithras, who is searching for his next disciple from within the modern British Army... and Mr Mkuzi, leader of a team of spiritual healers cleaning out a hospital's secret ward of shame.

Copies of Thomas's music back catalogue can be found on:
https://www.thomasmarty.bandcamp.com
or at www.bandcamp.com and search for ThomasMartyMusic

Ogam Tree Healing and Shamanic Healing:
www.martyshamanichealing.com

The Beginners Book of Ogam Tree Healing

'I am breath'

by

Thomas Marty

"Learn how to use Ogam tree healing energy for ourselves and others…"

Copyright © 2020 Thomas Marty

All rights reserved, including the right to reproduce this book, or portions thereof in any form. No part of this text may be reproduced, transmitted, downloaded, decompiled, reverse engineered, or stored, in any form or introduced into any information storage and retrieval system, in any form or by any means, whether electronic or mechanical without the express written permission of the author.

The views expressed in this work are solely those of the author and do not necessarily reflect the views of the publisher, and the publisher hereby disclaims any responsibility for them.

ISBN: 9798579148476

PublishNation
www.publishnation.co.uk

Medical Disclaimer

Please note that the information in this book should not be used as an alternative to orthodox medicine, nor as an alternative to doctor's or medical consultant's prescriptions, referrals, operations, advice, or treatment.

Ogam Tree Healing should be viewed as a complementary therapy – Ogam tree healing complements doctors and is not an alternative to them. Anyone with any illness should first see a doctor and accept the doctor's prescriptions, referrals, operations, advice or treatment.

You should not use any of these techniques or exercises if you are a UK citizen under the age of 18 or below the age of relevant legality or adulthood in the country in which you live or whilst driving or operating machinery or doing anything potentially hazardous.

Thomas Marty

Thomas Marty was born in 1959, in London. He has been a light worker for the last twenty-five years and has been extensively working as a Shamanic Practitioner since successfully passing his three-year training with the Sacred Trust. He is also a Practising Druid, a member of OBOD (Order of Bards, Ovates, and Druids) and a founder member of Corr Reisc (The Heron) Cambridge Druid Grove. Guided by Spirit, he has researched and explored the healing available via the Ogam trees and run many workshops that have helped to bring this book and way of working with healing nature to the wider domain.

Front cover design by Maya Marty

Etsy Shop: MayasillustrationArt

Acknowledgements and Thanks

My sincere thanks go to Yvette Marks for her encouragement, enthusiasm and help in creating this book. Her questioning of facts and prodding to make things clearer and a request to write from a more personal approach has helped make this book a more fun experience for me and hopefully for you. The secondary title, 'I am breath' comes from a Shamanic Journey Yvette undertook for me, where I asked the question, "What does Ogam Healing look like?" The answer was, "I Am Breath."

Thanks also to Susie Morris-Manuel for agreeing to host and find interested parties to come and experience the very first Ogam Tree Healing workshop. It was so important to share the information with others and get confirmation that this process works. We have a beautiful group that decided to meet more regularly between workshop sessions and meditate with the trees. It became a date to look forward to each week to meet and share experiences. My thanks also go to Sue Rhodes, Sue Bartlett, Anne Levinson, Charles Morris-Manuel, and Nina Ashby.

A special mention for my wife, Amanda, for putting up with my weekly disappearances into the woods and the long explanations of tree energies when we go together. She has had to put up with many pieces of bark, twigs, nuts and leaves that find their way home and take over the windowsills for weeks at a time. I should add that when I get into things, they tend to take over my life and I can't literally see the wood for the trees!

Special thanks also go to Nina Ashby and Amanda Marty for helping me edit this book. There have been many other people who I have shared this project with and all of them have been extremely positive and encouraging, I include some of the many case studies who were interested in receiving healing and were kind enough to agree to me using their experiences in this book. I'd like also to give great thanks to the Sacred Trust for starting me out on this new journey and OBOD, for its inspiration in exploring this work in earnest.

Chapters

Introduction	page 1
Dragons	page 6
Chapter 1 What is Ogam?	page 9
Chapter 2 What is Ogam Healing?	Page 16
Chapter 3 Spiritual Qualities of Nature	page 21
Chapter 4 Physical Interactions with Trees	page 24
Chapter 5 Creating Your Inner Grove	page 31
Chapter 6 Physical Healing	page 46
Chapter 7 Distant Healing	page 54
Chapter 8 Hand Positions for self and others	page 57
Chapter 9 Drawing the Symbols	page 61
Chapter 10 The Ogam Trees (Birch to Ash)	page 63
Chapter 11 The Ogam Trees (Hawthorn to Apple)	page 96
Chapter 12 The Ogam Trees (Vine to Elder)	page 133
Chapter 13 The Ogam Trees (Pine to Yew)	page 165
Chapter 14 The Ogam Forfeda (Grove to Beech)	page 200
Chapter 15 Preparing to Give Ogam Healing	page 227
Chapter 16 Biofeedback Sensations Explained	page 232
Chapter 17 Case Studies	page 237
Bibliography	page 246

Introduction

I became interested in all things spiritual when as a teenager my Higher Self began talking to me. This took place late at night when I was tucked up in bed going through the stresses and strains of growing up. It presented itself simply as a voice that softly called my name. Unfortunately, being brought up in a religion which saw any personal contact with God outside of the church as probably of a questionable origin, and the fact I owned a very active imagination, meant that I thought this voice was something far more sinister than it actually proved to be. My self-worth was very low at the time and it seemed to make sense that nothing *good* would ever be interested in me. I was also experiencing a number of psychic and supernatural events which only proved to me that I was being targeted by something nefarious.

A little later on when I eventually talked about it with my father, he recommended reading books on Edgar Cayce, a spiritual prophet in the 20th century. This resulted in being opened up to an exciting alternative view to conventional life and belief. A view that I could more naturally relate to and helped make sense of my strange experiences. From then onwards came the many rewarding years investigating the esoteric world. My spiritual life journey had begun in earnest. The right teachers appeared as if by magic at the right time and my dance with the universe and all its wonders continued to unfold in a beautiful symmetry.

After leaving drama school in the mid-80s, I had issues with my knees and decided to see if I could heal myself. I had, after all, read many books on self-healing. So, lying in my bed at night, I concentrated on bringing a white light down through my crown and into my knees. I remembered visualising a group of gnomes working hard at fixing the insides of my knees. I didn't know exactly what they were doing but they were hard at work and who was I to question them? Astonishingly, after a week of this, my knees did feel better. I could climb stairs without too much issue and no longer fell over after a long motor bike ride. Things were looking up and so I decided to go to a healing centre down on the South Coast for a long weekend of mind, body and soul healing.

I was introduced to sessions of spiritual healing, crystal healing, meditation, counselling, art therapy, aromatherapy and bathing in oils. Yes, I did feel better and my interest was completely aroused in the now intriguing and attractive world of complementary healing. During my acting career, in which I had a ball but also suffered many lows, my ego and personality was busily being tempered by the Gods for what was to come. There is no business, like show business, for that. There was still too much fear and self-doubt.

For the next fifteen years as well as my acting and creative life, I filled my spare time with many training courses (Reiki and Karuna healing, massage, reflexology, colour healing, spiritual healing, pranic healing, divination, magic, psychic development, working with angels, esoteric healing and astrology). I read a countless number of books and undertook much holistic research but always lurking in the background was the thought, *to what end?* Sure, my life was more peaceful, I was surrounded with good friends and I had met many fellow journey men and women who revealed themselves as signposts on the way, but certain things were missing, like a partner. I had given up looking by the age of thirty-four, it seemed that relationships and I were an impossibility and I take full blame for that. Then when I hit forty, I met my wife, moved to Cambridge and had three delightful children which meant that my eternal search for truth had to be put on a back burner for a short while whilst I concentrated on the responsibility of being a husband, father and earning a living (another version of truth in itself).

Running our own Theatre in Education Company with my wife and finding great success teaching and facilitating the many art projects that we developed in Cambridgeshire, helped rebuild my confidence and my fear of life started to fade. This newfound confidence continued to build for the next ten years and I successfully gained a degree in English Literature with the Open University. There was a cost to all this fantastic work, I realised that I was burning out and needed to change my focus. The Universe came to my aid via an old friend who offered me the opportunity of teaching drama at an international arts college. Within three years I had moved into the Welfare team and was trained as a counsellor. It would be true to say that during this time I couldn't totally keep away from my inner passion and had joined a psychic circle and trained with a number of other healing organisations.

Life was good and positive. Then one night, sitting alone I was thinking about things, as you do, when a new and attractive thought popped into my head, 'It's now time to look at Shamanic Healing.' It was as simple as that. I went on the web and searched for where I might find more information and the *Sacred Trust* website exploded onto my screen. As I read, there was a great excitement which took over my mind and body and I just knew that that was where I would need to study next.

After attending a number of weekend courses I applied for and was accepted onto their three year shamanic practitioner course. It took place in their excellent training centre in Dorset, set in beautiful countryside surroundings. Here in my first few days away I was asked to dig a grave and bury myself deep inside. This I diligently did and dug a hole at least five foot down, six feet long and three feet wide. I was urged to talk to Mother Earth about my life, the good, the bad and the ugly. It was at this moment I knew I had found my spiritual home and that my spiritual quest was on a whole new level. During this evening of harsh reality coming to face me, I was introduced to my Ancestor Clan, who are knowingly with me in all my work to this day.

In shamanism we are taught that spirit inhabits everything. Spirit is vibration and all matter vibrate at different rates to give us the many different physical manifestations around us. We too are included within this web of vibration, and once we understand this, we can see it and realise that communication is possible with all physical matter by tuning into the spirit that inhabits it. Whilst upon this training course we were asked, after one specific day's work, to find a tree that attracts you and to sit underneath it. Then to communicate with the spirit of the tree upon our day's experience. I found a tall pine tree which welcomed me to sit with my back against its trunk. Almost immediately I felt its spirit surround me and I wept. I introduced myself only to find it already knew all about me and had been waiting for the opportunity to converse. This we did. It was a conversation with an enlightened and sentient being. It answered many questions and posed some of its own, this book being in part an answer to one of them.

After graduating from the shamanic practitioner's course, I knew that I wished to work more closely with Mother Nature. I asked for guidance and was directed to work with the many ley lines that cross London and the South East. I would journey to each point, make contact with the spirit and offer healing which was always gratefully accepted. I set myself more projects to work with the land in as many ways I could and found myself travelling round the country to well-known stone circles, places of natural power and picking up new ways of healing the land as I went. My final project was journeying to many sites in Cambridge, both spiritually and physically, to get to know the spirit of the place and undertake healing for it. Not only did I get the pleasure of working with and for Mother Nature, I also managed to get around some pretty fantastic places too.

All this work was fine, but I wanted to gain more in-depth knowledge about the land and its ways, so I joined the Order of Bards, Ovates and Druids. The bard section helped me tune back into my creative side, so I wrote and published a book of short stories called *The Way of The World* and began writing my second book of slightly longer stories which was published in my Ovate year: *a little of what you fancy*. I am currently editing my first novel… I have recorded an album of self-penned songs with my good friend Tim Hooper and continue to write and play my music as and when I can.

My Ovate Grade found me out and about in my local nature reserve, which I affectionately call *the sanctuary*, and was introduced to Ogam. It was within the sanctuary I met with all the Ogam trees and created my personal link with them both in the physical and spiritual worlds.

As a Druid I am reaping more benefits than I ever thought possible. If shamanic training was the icing on the cake of my spiritual exploration, the Druid experience is highlighting the individual tastes of the ingredients within.

The *sanctuary* is on the edge of my home village, just outside of Cambridge. It has been here that I have been brought even closer to Mother Nature and the treasures that are available to us all. Walking in and interacting with nature, I have been opened up to the natural magical healing world we live in. I have seen not only the wide range of animal life which can be missed when growing up in the city, but the Fey and their workings, which if approached correctly, can be accessed too. For me, this time has been like becoming a child again, or retuning into that creative energy that never really leaves us. I wander round with my eyes now open, touching, tasting, smelling, feeling, hearing and interacting with the various lifeforms that are abundant in the world about us. The energy of the world and all its spiritual inhabitants is here for us to access by creating relationships, to help us change our personal lives for the better and heal the planet.

It was during a physical session with my first Ogam tree of choice, which happened to be an oak tree, that I was instructed to research into the healing aspects of each of the specific Ogam trees. This I did diligently for over a year and then undertook a number of case studies to practise the healing I had learnt. Many positive results came from this and so in January of 2020 I organised with my great shamanic practitioner colleague and friend, Susie Morris Manuel, my first teaching workshop. There were to be five one day courses in which we were to meet with the trees and connect with them. The results have been fantastic with many rich experiences gained by my first Ogam grove group. When we went into lockdown (due to the pandemic), we completed the last few workshops via zoom, which turned out to be just as successful. Not only have the students connected with the spirit and healing energies of the trees and deities, they have used them for healing themselves and others. This book is the culmination of two and a half years research work on the subject.

Dragons

In one of the first sessions at the Sacred Trust when learning to work with spiritual allies, I was approached by the dragons who told me that I needed to work with them. This was quite a mind-blowing request at the time, as I didn't have a clue what they were referring to and the fact that they are now very much part of my circle of allies has been a great positive in my development. Thankfully, I now understand much of what the dragons represent and offer us. On one shamanic pilgrimage to Cardiff Castle, more dragons appeared and became sacred entities to work with. Since then, they have made it quite clear that they hold much energy for the seeker to use in their spiritual work.

By tuning into the ancient ways of working with the land, its stones, plant, animal, human and spirit life, we have the opportunity to really experience all that is on offer in today's world. To retune into what has long been forgotten, misplaced or forbidden, gives it the added incentive of handling precious knowledge that is available to all. As the planet is presently suffering from our misuse of its properties, it is now time for us all to realize our responsibility and come together to heal it.

The dragons are more than just odd or formidable characters in fairy tales, they are and were in Celtic times associated with the power of the land. They can influence it and the land they frequent is possessed with special powers. The ancient Druids likened the earth to a body of a dragon and built stone circles on the power nodes of this body. They believed that dragons connected us with the earth's magnetism and healing waters. The Celts knew about the mysteries of ley lines (dragon lines), which are long lines of flowing cosmic energy running through the physical earth, normally in straight lines. Nowadays there are many books on them, and they have become pilgrim walks for those that wish to access them. You will notice upon these lines many ancient burial mounds, barrows, stone circles, sacred wells and springs and places of special significance. There are also many churches, which of course have been built upon the old pagan places of power. These were places where a dragon often passed or paused to rest thus making them more powerful and affecting the surrounding area.

Dragons have the ability of the gift of vision, wisdom and prophecy. They also were considered the guardians of all knowledge, wisdom and the treasures of the universe. It is interesting to note that in Celtic art, dragons were often depicted swallowing their own tails as if in a never-ending circle thus symbolizing eternal life and the cycle of life in nature. They were revered like gods bringing the heavenly and earth forces together. Dragons were also seen as guardians to the entrance way of both the Heavens and the Underworld.

There are two types of Celtic dragons, the usual four-legged, winged version and the sea serpent depicted as either a giant wingless serpent or giant serpent with wings but no legs. They were magnificent creatures that protected not only the earth but all living things upon it and were as natural to the physical world as mountains. It was only after Christianity came to these shores that dragons were demonized as symbols of trouble, strife and infertility being depicted as evil and a symbol of the devil. For the Celts the dragons were considered the most powerful symbol of all.

The dragons that made themselves known to me have disclosed that they can be used to represent the five elements. How apt then to come full circle and re-use the dragons as they were originally intended, as power symbols to help heal the earth and all upon it. When working with the elements, I have been blessed with five named dragons to use as additional power symbols with the Ogam energy. The time is right to reintroduce ourselves to their energy and use it to heal ourselves and the neglected and badly disfigured land we live in. Let us not forget that we are linked to it. We are as apples on a tree that grows on the land. If we destroy it, the tree will die and there will no longer be any apples! By raising our energy up and using it for positive purposes we can magically reconnect with the heavenly forces that never ever left but have been waiting in the wings for us to come to our senses and once again access them as a positive force. For those of you who are used to using the usual symbols of Hawk, Stag, Salmon and Bear, the Arch Angels or even the North American symbols for the elements and you feel more comfortable using these symbols, please feel free to continue to do so.

1

What is Ogam?

The Ogam script consists of a set number of letters or symbols which have a horizontal or vertical line with shorter lines that are either centred on or branch off from it. There are five groups each made up of five symbols, the fifth group was added much later in history, see below for details. It is worth noting that up until now, Ogam energy has been used mainly for divination and meditational purposes.

These symbols have survived down to modern day as inscriptions on stones that can still be found in Ireland, Wales, Scotland and England. We also have information about its use in The Scholar's Primer from Scotland, which was transcribed from the oral tradition in the 17th century and O'Flaherty's Ogygia from Ireland which was published in 1793. It was brought into the public domain in 1948 by Robert Graves in his book called The White Goddess. It is not an easy language to write but it is in its symbolism where it really comes alive. There are many theories concerning its history, most inscriptions can be dated back to the 5th or 6th century, but most people see it coming from even further back, as pre-Celtic in origin and perhaps as a tool of Druid wisdom.

Ogam, when seen as the ancient alphabet of the Druids, links each letter to a specific tree. Trees are universal, archetypal symbols that were used in many of the ancient traditions. They are also a spiritual and sacred symbol for rebirth, physical and spiritual growth, union, transformation, liberation, sustenance and fertility. Underlying all tree work is the understanding that nature is the visible face of spirit. Trees play an extraordinary role in spirituality. They have been held sacred in both ancient and modern cultures. They are beautiful, symbolic and a source of natural energy both in the physical and spiritual world.

Those of us that work with trees, see them as treasure chests with their own medicines, spiritual power and divination gifts.

The word Ogam refers only to the form of letters or script, while the letters themselves are known collectively as the Beith-luis-nuin after the letter names of the first letters. The Ogam alphabet originally consisted of twenty distinct characters (feda), arranged in four groups of aicme. Each aicme was named after its first character, as in; aicme beith, aicme huath, aicme muin, aicme ailim. There were five additional letters which were later introduced and called the forfeda. The twenty standard letters of the Ogam alphabet and the five forfeda are as follows:

B beith: Silver Birch: This symbol represents new beginning, change, purity and rebirth.

L luis: Rowan: The symbol represents protection, insight and control.

F fearn: Alder: This symbol represents strong spiritual foundation and principles. It also is linked with oracular powers.

S saille: Willow: The symbol represents spiritual growth and knowledge wisely applied. A strong feminine influence brings you healing and protection.

N nuin: Ash: The symbol represents the connection between the inner self to the outer worlds. A symbol of creativity and all that transitions between these points.

H huath: Hawthorn: The symbol represents the cleansing, protection and fertility.

D duir: Oak: The symbol represents the strength, the doorway to wisdom and self-confidence.

T tinne: Holly: This symbol represents courage, balance and power.

C coll: Hazel: This symbol represents wisdom, creativity and enlightenment.

Q quert: Apple: This symbol represents love, choice and rebirth.

M muin: Vine: This symbol represents prophecy, truth and inner development.

G gort: Ivy: This symbol represents tenacity, growth and both physical and spiritual development.

NG ngetal: Reed: This symbol represents direct action, healing and communication.

S straif: Blackthorn: This symbol represents authority, control and power.

R ruis: Elder: This symbol represents transition, maturity and change.

A ailim: Pine: This symbol represents clarity of vision, awareness and understanding.

O ohn: Furze: This symbol represents determination, collecting and passion.

U ur: Heather: This symbol represents generosity, healing and success.

E eadha: Aspen: This symbol represents endurance, courage and self-confidence.

I idho: Yew: This symbol represents transition, endings and change.

The Forfeda

The Forfeda is the fifth aicme of the Ogam system and was added after the Greek language came to Ireland. The people using Ogam needed other symbols for the diphthongs and extra sounds in Greek and so the forfeda was added.

As you may know and depending on your point of view, there are different associations and meanings for these extra five symbols. I have used specific tree options where possible. Whilst these additional letters are not to be found on the stone inscriptions and sparsely used in manuscripts, they were part of medieval Ogam tradition and therefore up for development and use in the twenty-first century. My choice for this forfeda are as follows:

Ea koad/grove: This symbol represents communication, resolution and justice.

Oi oire: Spindletree: This symbol represents community relationships, revelations and honour.

Ui uillean: Honeysuckle: This symbol represents manifesting of will, pathway to inner search and secrets.

Io/Ia iphin: Gooseberry: This symbol represents abundance, success, meeting your needs, sharing with others, stepping out of your comfort zone.

Ae eamhancholl: Beech: This symbol represents ancient knowledge, insight and learning.

The Druids placed the trees into one of three categories which were ranked to their value as a crop. It was also a good way to stop people from illegally felling them with distinct penalties for each of the specific categories.

Chieftain:

Alder, Ash, Oak, Hazel, Vine, Ivy, Blackthorn, Yew, Mistletoe, Furze, Beech.

Peasant:

Birch, Rowan, Willow, Hawthorn, Holly, Heather, Spindle, Honeysuckle.

Shrub:

Apple, Reed, Elder, Fir, Aspen.

The Deities

Within my research I have discovered the many deities associated with the individual Ogam trees. These deities can help us access the tree energy and explore the qualities in new ways. It would be right to inform you now that Neptune has come forward to me as the main God of Ogam Healing. His symbol is that of the trident and there is more on this later in the book, including how to draw all symbols.

Sacred Grove

A sacred grove is a grove of trees which has special religious importance to different cultures. They were used as open-air woodland temples by cultures stretching across the world in which they were and still are used for meetings, teaching, celebrating, healing and much more. For this book's purposes we will be creating our own sacred grove in spirit, to access Ogam tree healing energy for our needs.

How to Access and Use the Ogam Symbols

Each tree has its own specific energy vibration (level) and by linking in with it, we can learn to channel its innate energy. It is best to first access it spiritually from our inner grove. Once there, we journey to our intended tree and merge with the spirit within by drawing its symbol in our top 5 chakras. Once we have attuned ourselves to this energy, we can then visit the tree in physical reality and channel energy from it also.

The physical and spiritual worlds both have their own virtues and when we combine them, it can really enhance the experience. An elder brother who taught me many years ago, used to say, "Live in both worlds more, rather than one world less." *Intention* is the key for success and a willing to spend your time both in the silence and the great outside. When working on others, we will find that not only can we work on them physically in our healing space but send healing over any distance.

Tree Energy

Trees act as a source for energy on many levels:

Physical: The peace, shelter, warmth and security of walking, sitting, accessing it in nature, and the eating of its fruit and nuts. The using of it in our building of houses, boats and machines and finally the warmth and cooking possibilities it provides as a raw resource.

Emotional: The fun we have whilst walking through a wood, climbing trees or calmness whilst warming ourselves at a tree's feet or by a small fire in a glade.

Mental: Calmness of mind when in the company of nature and trees in general.

Spiritual: We can access healing, divination, meditational, and magical communication with the spirit that inhabits the tree. It is possible to aid our spiritual development through interaction with nature.

Each individual tree, like all living things has an energy frequency/ vibrational note and an aura. The roots give it great grounding deep in the ground. The vibration is generally an energy of safety, security and stability. When interacting with a tree, realise that you are all these things too. Please remember to be respectful, so send it some loving energy back and always give your thanks. This will help to ensure a positive and growing relationship.

2

What is Ogam Healing?

Ogam Healing is using life force energy via the prism of specific trees, for healing purposes. Each type of tree has an individual symbol which gives access to the energies associated with it. This energy can be used to heal yourself, others, plants, animals or situations. It can also inspire you to connect with your higher self, receive direct revelation, practice divination, bring peaceful repose through meditation, use in magic, link into your creativity and change your life for the better.

What Is Ogam Tree Energy?

It is made up of life force energy (highest spiritual energy or consciousness) and has the potential to know who needs what type of healing energy, when and how. It exists in the higher planes and inner planes of Spirit and that is why we create an inner grove of trees to help source it. By following the guide to self-attunement in this book, you too can access this energy. By attuning yourself, it gives you the autonomy and control to use these energies and explore wisely. This life force energy promotes physical, emotional, mental and spiritual balance. Ogam can help return imbalance to normal.

Who Can Learn Ogam Healing?

Anyone can learn this form of Ogam healing. All you need is the patience, practice and desire to do so. The ability comes through your link with the symbols themselves by placing them in the specific higher chakras.

Benefits In Learning Ogam Healing

Self-healing (renews your life force energy)

Healing family members (with their permission)

Healing friends (with their permission)

Healing animals or pets

Keeping illness at bay – staying in wholeness (power-full)

Increasing existing knowledge

Developing your psychic abilities

Enhancing your spiritual nature

Finding your personal soul path

Healing the physical, emotional, mental and spiritual states

Seeking enlightenment

Working with the land

Healing the land

Learning distant healing methods

Specifics

Ogam can reduce or eliminate pain

It can renew your life force energy

It treats stress related disorders

It brings about deep relaxation, grounds you and helps stimulate the body's metabolism and detoxification systems

Ogam can be used on the physical, emotional, mental and spiritual bodies of a client

Ogam can be used in a distant healing way and set to be received at a different time from when the healing session takes place (Spirit works outside the confines of the three-dimensional world)

Ogam can help you transform your life

How Long Does It Take To Learn?

The sooner you create the Ogam grove of trees in the inner world and meet and work with the spirits of the trees, the sooner you will feel the benefits. It depends upon the individual wishing to investigate and explore the power of Ogam healing. It is up to you!

Experiencing Ogam Healing

You can experience Ogam healing by channelling its energy directly, through meditation, or communing with the Ogam trees in this physical reality. During this event, people often report various feelings of warmth or coolness, itchy-ness, pins and needles or a sense of bubbling energy movement (see biofeedback sensations explained section), or nothing. Some experience colours, the presence of spiritual beings, have visions but most people experience deep relaxation and peace. Some fall soundly asleep.

How Is an Ogam Treatment Given?

You can use Ogam healing for yourself, or others. For the sake of simplicity, the person who is receiving Ogam healing in this book is named *the client recipient*. An Ogam treatment is usually given in a quiet and peaceful environment with the client either lying or sitting down. The practitioner will channel the Ogam energy whilst placing their hands either on or over various points of the client's body. A treatment can last between 30 minutes to an hour. There is no need to remove any items of clothes apart from shoes, if on a couch. You can also use distant healing, intention being the key. We are far more powerful than we imagine.

You might also lead your client through a meditation where they create their own Ogam grove and journey to the tree of choice and sit within its power. Then you call for the specific energy you want to channel down through them.

Attunements

It is in the process of self-attunement that Ogam healing energy can be channelled. Please see section later in the book, but in a nutshell, it is about creating an Ogam grove within your inner mind/inner plane/spirit world and by use of the symbol of each tree accessing the spirit energy within.

Once you have connected with the spirit energy, you should place the symbol both physically and mentally in your top five major spiritual chakras (including your *spirit gate*, located at the back of your neck). Then place the symbol in the palms of your hands and souls of the feet. Once attuned to a specific Ogam tree, you need only tune into the symbol to unlock the energies you are seeking to use for healing.

21 Day Clearing Process

It is not unusual for some people to start a clearing process after their self-attunements or self-healings, which can last from a few days to a few weeks. This clearing can be physical, mental or emotional. Ogam energy begins to heal and balance you on all levels. Toxins that have built up in your body now begin to be gently removed. Trapped emotional energy is released and you may feel angry, weepy or feel tired. After this has passed you may move into the positive reactions, which include increased clarity of thought, better concentration, memory etc...

Once attuned to Ogam healing energy, you only have to place your hands on yourself, another person, animal or plant with the intention to heal and the healing energy will flow. I regularly have sessions not only with humans and situations, but have also healed horses, dogs and my cat. His reactions never fail to amaze me. For the first month it is recommended to tune into the energy on a daily basis.

Channelling

What is important is to remember that you are acting as a channel for the Ogam healing energy to enter in a focussed way into the life of the person you are healing. Remember Ogam is not religious. You are not the source of healing, the divine is. That is why giving treatments does not drain you personally. During an Ogam session, both you and the client are being treated because the Ogam energy balances you as well as the person you are healing.

3

Spiritual Qualities of Nature

Symbiotic relationships are a special type of interaction between species. Sometimes beneficial, sometimes harmful, these relationships are essential to many organisms and ecosystems, and they provide a balance that can only be achieved by working together.

This is called Mutualism: both partners benefit.

Humans breathe out carbon dioxide, trees breath it in, they breathe out oxygen, and humans breathe that in. So on and so forth… We are both linked to the ground which we come from and receive our nutrients. We both have spiritual links and therefore can interact to send and receive healing, knowledge and energy. All parts of the physical collective world which include, the land, plants, animals, and humans are alive, interrelated and exist at varying vibrational rates. These states of matter exist in two forms, the physical as we see and interact with every day, and the invisible world of spirit.

Within this form, we humans have an etheric body surrounding the physical body acting as an energy form linking it to the emotional body, wherein our emotional feelings are played out. Around that form comes the mental body where our thoughts exist, and gives access to our Higher Self, from then onwards the subtle spiritual bodies reach out, touching one another in a more energetic way, linking us all together with all that is, and finally to the source of all life; the divine.

The thing to understand is that all these bodies/worlds/ interpenetrate each other much as gas, water and solids do in the physical world. The premise of how life exists is that within our own physical world we also have the worlds of the astral (emotional), mental and spiritual worlds interconnected, living, being and having their expression. The structure of life as we know it, including cell growth, structure and expression are all able to have direct influence from these subtler worlds. At this point it is important to note that each living thing therefore has access to higher life forms or energies that can be channelled through to it by various means. Thought, emotions, direct channelling, and touch.

Our own subtler bodies can become more refined and attuned to these specific energies, especially when we train ourselves in how to contact and use these levels of perception. How do we do this? By simply taking the time to recognise that these levels exist and tune into them often through meditation, dream-work, prayer or direct links with the spiritual entities that exist in these worlds.

If we look at the many indigenous tribes who have existed at varying times upon this planet, they have usually had direct and constant intercourse with these other worlds and the entities within them. The modern tribes seem to be hanging on with their fingernails to their cultural ways. They have lived with the spirits in a marriage which suited both sides and enjoyed a life full of meaning; the shaman who would direct his tribe to water and food sources whilst nomadically moving round the vast expanses of land, the medicine men/women deep in the jungle/forests who interact with the plant life so as to have a perfectly natural medicine cabinet that never runs empty at their side, the healers who channel energy to help change the vibrational rate inside a person, animal and plant to help bring it back into what is called a natural energy state of body, mind and spirit. The farmers who worked with the spirit of the land to grow their crops in traditional and sometimes formidable circumstances. There are also the weather workers, who can call up the rain when needed and keep it away when not. Psychopomp healers who move on stuck entities from all the different energy levels to where they need to be and back to the shamanic practitioners who bring back part of the human soul essence which has fled due to trauma.

When we are well and firing on all cylinders, we are power-full. When weak and dis-eased, we are power-less. By filling ourselves with healing energy, we once again can start our journey back to becoming full of power.

In this Ogam healing workbook we are looking at how we can work with specific trees to access their healing energy which they are happy to give freely. We will also learn how to flex our spiritual muscles to be able to develop our contact with our own spiritual higher nature and therefor benefit. Before we do this, let us look at building a link with the tree energy in the physical world.

4

Physical Interactions with Trees

Trees have probably been around you since you were born. You might have climbed them, hidden behind or within them and collected their fruit and nuts for games and to eat. It recently became fashionable for people to hug trees and is done for many different reasons culminating in many books being written about tree communication. The proof of the pudding is in the eating, as they say. There are however several methods to use when choosing to contact the spirit of the physical tree. Please remember that these living plants do have a spirit within them and that just like some humans, aren't too keen to be hugged out of the blue, climbed upon or shouted at. They are as diverse as you and me, which means that they will have access to variants of the energy associated to that tree. However, should you wish to respect it as a living sentient being, here is some guidance that can help you create a strong and harmonious bond between you both.

Try to be as open and respectful as you can. Before approaching them, let them know you are coming and what your intention is. Stop a good twenty feet away and through a prayer of introduction, let them know who you are and what you want from them. If you feel that you have been accepted, move on up and sit at the base of the trunk. Sit in its energy and take your time to feel it. It can manifest as tingling, hot or cold spots of energy, you may get dizzy, feel totally relaxed or feel nothing. Sit in its energy so it can feel and tune into yours. Remember this is a two-way scenario.

I recently travelled to Wales to work with my good friend and shamanic practitioner Yvette Marks. She took me to meet with the oldest Yew tree in the UK or quite possibly the whole of

Europe. It is said to be over five thousand years young. I stopped twenty feet from it and relaxed as I have learnt to do. Immediately I felt welcomed and the Yew spoke to me as an old friend would. I was invited into its space and to meet both aspects of it. It exists as two main trees, one almost distinct from the other. We laughed and joked about little things and he let me walk about it and take pictures. His sister tree also interacted with just as much friendship and love. The Fey were very present in and around the tree and the energy was amazing to feel. Both invited me to come back by shamanic journey practice and visit them again.

Time is observed slightly differently by trees and if you wish to create a lasting relationship with one or more, make sure you visit regularly to develop a positive one. Once a relationship develops, it can be like meeting an old friend. Should you wish for a physical part of the tree for your work, ask for a gift from the tree, or root about underneath it and see what you can find. Sometimes the tree will offer you gifts of its bark, twigs, fruit or flowers from its trunk and branches, please only take what you need. Potential wands, divining rods as well as nuts and fruit can often be found at the base of trees after a strong wind has passed by. Ask and you shall receive. An offering of water, mead, honey or a prayer will always be gratefully accepted.

Physical Tree Healing

When making spiritual communication with a tree, you may find that it is on a very subtle level. Let it be tender and understand that you may not be the one in charge of the situation so don't fight for control. Trees are welcoming and once a relationship has developed, they are just as inquisitive of you, as you are of them. You may also find that they know all about you as we carry our life stories about in our auras which can be read and understood by those in the know.

Relax and let yourself sink and merge into communication. This might be visual, whereas you see the spirit of the tree appear in a way that suits you. I tend to see them in my mind's eye as

Druids, or feminine spirits (Dryads). I have been welcomed into the trunks of trees, to climb down some steps and sit with the spirit of the tree across a table, or just become as part of the tree itself and then commenced to chat about all sorts of things. Sometimes it is a fleeting thought, or brush of positive energy touching your hair or cheek. My favourite time was when my local oak blessed me on my very first visit by dripping some of its resin onto me. You do not have to ask anything from them but just enjoy their wonderful company.

Should you have some questions ready, try not to make them closed, as in, yes and no ones. Ask for example, 'What are the benefits of....?' 'When would be a good time to...?' 'Please explain why these things happen to me?' Remember that once you have asked your question, be open minded, open hearted and accept that these spirits are all loving and working on a higher plane. You may get direct revelation or be treated to a symbolic/ metaphoric picture show.

Should you request a healing, make sure that again you ask respectfully. If you get one, great. Relax and enjoy it. If not, remember that the time may not be right for them to undertake this healing and from a spiritual point of view, you might be experiencing dis-ease as a learning experience. We don't always get what we want, we get what we deserve. Please do not challenge or threaten the tree or even get annoyed if you do not receive what you expect.

Using the Ogam Symbol in the Company of a Physical Ogam Tree.

It helps to know exactly why and what you want healing for. But be prepared for change as spirit can often see things that might need attention in advance of what you suspect is the case. A little humble acceptance of how spirit works should be acknowledged too. In each tree section you will find a list of issues/ illnesses/ diseases which can be healed by that tree. This list is not finite, and you might find more possibilities through your own research work.

Note that it is best to have attuned yourself to the tree's symbol in the spiritual before trying to access it in the physical. Once you have achieved this, please follow the order as indicated:

- Choose what it is you want to work on at this moment in time for yourself and go out and find where the tree associated with it, is located.

- Approach the tree with respect.

- Tune into the spirit of the tree you are with.

- Once contact has been made, draw the appropriate Ogam symbol and tune into its energy (using your mind's eye or fingers - the order of line strokes is provided in later in this book).

- Whilst you are doing this, make your intention strong and simple (e.g. I call in the power of Hawthorn to heal my heart).

- Do not reinforce your illness by saying, 'I have heart disease, please heal that.' By using these words or words like it, you will only reinforce that (illness) energy within you. Better to ask for... 'cell repair and healthy love to heal the cells in my... (affected area).'

- Now sit and feel the energy filling you up on the inside, coming through your crown chakra into your heart and also surrounding you. It might feel different to each of us, but usually can feel like hotness, coldness, tingles, electricity, pulses, wind... or indeed sometimes like nothing.

- The energy being channelled might work in waves or in circles and you might find that your body or head starts to move accordingly with the flow of this energy. Go with the flow.

- See/feel this energy flowing directly to the point/s needed and working on the area.

- Keep the intention flowing in your mind and keep it positive, "I am channelling healing Hawthorn energy, for the greatest and highest good of all concerned."

- If your mind wanders, note it and bring it back online. Do not scold yourself or give yourself a hard time. It is sometimes difficult to keep our minds focused. There are times that this is of benefit to us as the energy will flow regardless with us 'out of the way.' There is a suggestion list of visualisations/chants etc later in the book to help at these times.

- Once you feel/know or are told that time is up, disengage and give thanks for the healing that has taken place. Open your eyes and rub your hands round your body to bring yourself totally back into the physical world. Take some time to appreciate what has just happened and take your time to leave the tree.

- It is sometimes advisable to have someone on hand to help get you back home, especially if you have travelled a distance to your chosen tree.

- It is always good to leave an offering for the tree.

Tree Parts

You might also like to try working with any tree parts you have managed to collect from your travels into the natural world. Once you have the physical part in your hands, you need to activate or tune in with the spirit of the tree which exists within it. Do not be fooled by thinking a piece of bark, twig, flower or leaf holds no power. It does. Tune into the spirit of the tree through that axis mundi and its energy will come to you. I do this weekly with my divination work, by tuning into a piece of alder bark, donated to me by the tree. It has never failed me yet. I also have a length of oak bark that I use when I want to channel strength or courage into a project. It works.

When asking for divine guidance, understand that spirit can communicate through many mediums including speech, thoughts, visions, feelings, tastes, smells and touch. The answer to your questions may come later in the day when you hear it in the words of a song, within the writings of a book, or an advert on TV. Be open to however it comes your way and especially look out for synchronicities which is a good way of realising things are working for you.

Note of Caution

As I have said above, each physical tree will have varying amounts of the qualities attributed to that species. Some have more power than others, some may not even want to help you – it's not a written law that all nature should bow down to man. That is why we not only work with the spirit of the physical tree, when allowed, but also bring in the link we have made with our individual spiritual Ogam grove, tracing the tree's symbol in our chakras. That way, you get double bubble when all is positive.

What if you do not have any of these trees around you where you live?

Not all of us are blessed with having access to the trees we would like to meet. You might wish to make a special event out of travelling across cities hunting them down, looking at maps to discover your nearest park, open space, or wasteland. Go for explorative walks down avenues or boulevards where trees line them.

Within this book there is a lot of information on each tree and should you wish to know more, google it. Look at the images on your computer. There is nothing better than when coming across a tree you know, to have sudden bits of information flow into your consciousness. They can be treated as old friends and by giving them a blessing as you pass by, will only strengthen your links to it and nature as a whole. If possible, a walk in nature every day will help to bring immense healing benefits to us. Should this be impossible, then access the energies of these trees via your inner Ogam grove.

5

Creating Your Inner Grove

Why do we need to do this? To create a portal for access to the spiritual energies in the inner world. It also becomes a place to meet and greet your allies and the deities. It is an opportunity to channel their energies and conduct our healing work. I also suggest you start a journal to write your experiences up, to record any messages from Spirit and in time your own healing sessions. Please undertake this practice in a private and quiet space, free from any distractions.

Attunement with the Spirits/symbols of the Trees

We will attune ourselves with each tree's energy by using the following meditations. We attune ourselves to the energy of each Ogam tree by merging with its energy in our grove whilst drawing its specific symbol into the following chakra points in our bodies; the crown, third eye, spirit gate, throat, heart and the palms of the hand and soles of the feet.

Feel the energy flow through you and observe your reactions to this energy. Once you are connected, you are attuned to this energy and tree. We draw the symbols into our palms, for there are smaller chakra points here too, and can channel the energy through our hands into ourselves or our clients. We use the soles of our feet to help ground into earth energy and pull it in through our feet, also we can tune into the roots of the trees in our grove and root in with them.

Chakra Information

The word chakra comes from the Sanskrit language, meaning *wheel*. The chakras are centres of energy and it is through them that we draw in energy for the benefit of our bodies. They should be kept clear and protected from negative influences for us to remain healthy. There are seven major centres which we will focus on for now and of course the lesser-known Spirit Gate.

Chakras are whirling energy vortices that vary in size and speed of revolution. When we fail to address life's problems, we fail to process the energies involved and store the negative energy created in the subtle bodies, especially the chakras; these then become blocked and slow down. The result is physical/ mental / emotional disorder and disease. When one chakra becomes blocked this has an effect in its neighbouring chakras – creating a state of overload in them as well.

The lower three chakras relate to what is often called the lower self, i.e. the basic appetites, needs, conditional emotions and lower mental functions, whilst the upper three relate to the spiritual. These are balanced by the heart or 4th chakra.

The chakras are believed to link directly to the endocrine system which controls hormone production throughout the body, which is particularly important in maintaining homeostasis (balance and harmony). Blockages in the chakras result in a variety of mental and physical disorders. One of the roles of the healer is to balance the centres and channel through them the healing energy that will facilitate self-healing.

The chakras are linked to a network of fine lines running throughout our bodies rather like our veins and arteries. These are called the Meridians. They are pathways or energy channels believed to be related to the internal organs of the body. They were documented in China around 400BC in Nei Ching Su Wen which means The Yellow Emperor's Classic of Internal Medicine. The meridians carry the essential life force known as

Chi, Ki or Nwyfre. If the Meridian network is blocked, then the life force cannot flow, and disease follows.

As well as the 7 largest Chakras there are thought to be 360 of them over the body, strategically positioned to link the energetic activity of the etheric and the physical. Many of the chakra points also coincide with acupuncture points.

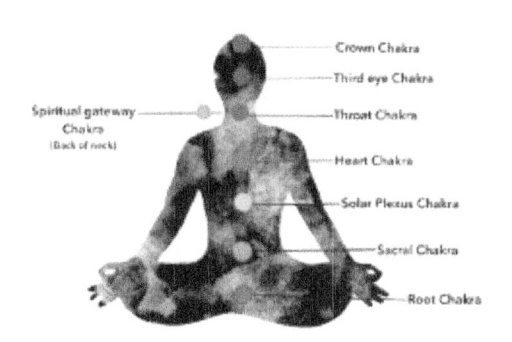

Chakra Energies

The 3 centres located in the lower part of the body; base, sacral and solar plexus are related to the basic human needs and those located in the upper regions are related to the spiritual; heart, throat, brow and crown. The spirit gate is located at the back of the neck and is the doorway to spiritual dimensions.

The following are a guide to the main chakras (including the lesser-known spirit gate) which we are interested in, they all relate to one another and interact with each other.

Base Centre:

Colour red or rose pink in the older or very spiritual person.

The connection with the earth and physical reality. It controls the base of the spine and the flow of the physical and creative energy through the body. It has a close relationship with the etheric body. Some say it controls the gonads.

Sense: Smell

Affects: The lower pelvis, hips, legs, feet (skeleton and muscles)

Deals with fear of sexuality, fear of the world, lack of confidence, survival, aggression and self-defence.

Sacral or Abdominal Centre:

Its basic colour is orange.

This centre works closely with the base and solar plexus as it sits between them. It controls the lower digestive system and the wellbeing of the adrenals. For hormones to be released and balanced as they should be, this centre needs to be functioning well.

Sense: Taste

Body: Etheric (the power body that immediately surrounds the physical body and connects to the astral or emotional body)

Affects: Testes, ovaries, womb, kidneys, lower back, colon, sensitivity and social interaction.

Deals with low esteem, self-love, creativity, sexuality and joy of the inner child.

Solar Plexus:

Colour yellow and linked to the pancreas area.

The centre is important in many ways and is concerned with a person's individuality. It reflects your state of mind and intellectual attitude to life and links in with the left side of the brain. Many people see a link with the adrenals due to the fight or flight action of the solar plexus. Fear and anxiety register here and because of the link to the left-hand side of the brain, thought becomes action. Medically it indicates disharmony in the liver and the pancreas. The centre frequently needs healing or cleansing as it is a centre of reaction and a storehouse for tension.

Sense: Sight.

Body: Astral (emotional body)

Affects: The entire energy system, adrenals, time and space, digestion, pancreas, liver, breathing, gall bladder, middle back.

Heart Centre:

Colour Green.

Linked in at the centre of your chest, above the heart. The heart centre is the link between the basic human needs and the spiritual aspects of the person. It reflects the emotions and reveals how the person relates to others and to nature. It is important to the health of the heart and is a centre which is easily abused by alcohol, drugs and smoking. Excessive emotional tendencies are harmful to this centre. It is the centre of love and compassion, reflecting how the person relates to self, to others, to nature and the planet.

Sense: Touch

Body: Feeling

Affects: Heart, lungs, middle and upper back, arms and hands.

Deals: threats to belief patterns, emotional problems, inner-feelings, unconditional love and the soul.

Throat Centre:

Colour Pale Blue.

Linked in at the region of the thyroid to which it relates. From this centre the person expresses the whole being and communicates in a variety of ways and at different levels of being. The throat centre also relates to the throat itself, to the lungs, the respiratory and bronchial systems. Blocks can be created here and cause neck and shoulder problems. Many people suffer tensions in this area.

Sense: Hearing

Body: Mental

Affects: Self-expression, communication, creativity, trust, thyroid, ears, nose and throat.

Spirit Gate:

Colour Turquoise.

Found at the back of the neck. This chakra point acts as an energetic doorway through which we can communicate spiritually with other dimensions. It is also known as the Alta Major chakra. When attempting to attune to higher spiritual energies, it is through this portal that they can be reached.

Brow Centre:

Colour Indigo

Sometimes called the third eye or ajna, located between your eyebrows (forehead), but is associated with the pineal gland further back in the brain. When open and well worked it will wake up your intuition and inner wisdom. The pineal gland is linked and acts as a lock on the pituitary gland which is the master gland of the endocrine system. A very important centre, it is related to the right side of the brain and to intuition. Memories are stored here so it could be referred to as the computer of the energy system. Sensitivity and disharmony can both be registered here; it could be said to be important in the balance (homeostasis) of the energy system.

Sense: Psychic

Body: Higher mental

Affects: Intuition, planning, clairvoyance, face, brain, eyes and head.

Deals: Lower chakras, knowledge of past lives, reason.

Crown Centre:

Colour Violet

Linked in at the pineal gland or seat of the soul. It is the seat of consciousness and the doorway to source/divinity. It is essential that this centre opens or activates in the attunement process for healing and meditation. The crown centre is often described as the thousand petalled lotus. One of the roles of the healer is to balance the centres and channel through them the healing energy which will facilitate self-healing. Harmonious well-balanced centres will create a well-balanced person.

Sense: Spiritual

Body: Soul

Affects: Brain, entire physical body, unity, complete functioning.

Deals: Shock, trauma, all spiritual matters.

Creating Your Inner Grove

Now follow the next few steps. It's probably better to read them through a couple of times so you can see how it all works before attempting it.

Warning: Please don't try these meditations whilst driving, working with machines or walking down the road. It is a practice to be undertaken whilst sitting or lying in a comfortable and safe environment. Your spine should be straight, and body relaxed. If you are suffering severe mental health issues, please check that this process will be of benefit to you and not cause further distress.

Beginning

You might like to light a candle, use incense or use music, drum/rattle to heighten the vibration you are about to experience, or indeed you might prefer silence. To get the most out of these meditations, you might to record your version of it to listen through headphones.

Meditation One: Creating your Grove

Please take three deep breathes to help you relax the body and calm the mind. Follow each breath in for three counts, hold for one count and then exhale slowly out through your mouth. Each breath brings you into a more relaxed state of being. If stray thoughts wander into your mind at any point, note them and let them go without judgement. Follow the next breath in and follow it down into your lungs, feel them expand, count to three and then allow your mind to follow the expelled air out of your mouth. Have a quick check around your body, inside and out, looking for any stiffness or tension and should you find any, take your time to relax that area. Readjust the body should it need it and finally let your jaw drop slightly open and feel your face relax.

Perhaps let a wry smile cross your face as you take your third deep breath in and let it naturally out when it feels right to do so.

Sensing yourself dropping deeper, deeper and deeper still, relaxing both the mind and body until you feel you are ready to move onwards...

Now focussing your attention into the centre of your chest and sense, see and feel a ball of white light spark alight within your heart chakra. Let it expand gradually in size until it fills your whole chest with a beautiful, loving, peaceful energy. See it growing ever larger, taking in your throat chakra, spirit gate chakra, third eye chakra and finally your crown chakra. This peaceful, calming energy also travels downwards, taking in your solar plexus chakra, sacral chakra and base chakra...

Sit within this energy for a few moments, feeling yourself powering up. Then let the ball of white light expand further, downwards past your feet and into the ground below, rooting and grounding yourself into earth energy. You are being held safely in both the spirit world and physical world. See yourself completely immersed in this great ball of powerful spiritual white light, protected, empowered and linked directly into Divine energy...

Now it is time to journey to your grove. Speak the following intention, "My intention is to journey to my grove, my intention is to journey to my grove, my intention is to journey to my grove."

See yourself walking along a grassy path and ahead of you is a beautiful gate which will lead you directly into your grove. Sense the power of the place, see the many trees that surround this grove, and which are spreading out across the landscape. At the gate is the Guardian of the grove. They welcome you, opening the gate to let you enter and as you do you feel the true power of this grove fill you with wonder, expectation and love. For here you are as safe as you can be, here you can interact and meet with your spiritual allies, deities, ancestors and teachers. Here magic truly resides. Spend a short time with your guardian, ask their name, ask for them to show you round the inner grove or simply sit in silent contemplation...

It is time to bring in the elements to help power up your grove. Turn to the direction opposite your gate and face the East. Call in the Great Air Dragon, 'Fathross the Yellow, Fathross the Yellow, Fathross the Yellow, welcome to my sacred space, sacred grove and sacred healing.' Witness a large yellow dragon entering your grove. Spend a few moments sitting in its energy…

Now turn to your right, face the South and let us call in the Great Fire Dragon, 'Idreth the Red, Idreth the Red, Idreth the Red, welcome to my sacred space, sacred grove and sacred healing.' Witness a large red dragon entering your grove. Spend a few moments sitting in its energy…

Now turn to your right, face the West and let us call in the Great Water Dragon, 'Icress the Blue, Icress the Blue, Icress the Blue, welcome to my sacred space, sacred grove and sacred healing.' Witness a large blue dragon entering your grove. Spend a few moments sitting in its energy…

Now turn to your right, face the North and let us call in the Great Earth Dragon, 'Mordreth the Green, Mordreth the Green, Mordreth the Green, welcome to my sacred space, sacred grove and sacred healing.' Witness a large green dragon entering your grove. Spend a few moments sitting in its energy…

Now face upwards towards the heavens and let us call in the Great Spirit Dragon, 'Dwyfer the Black, Dwyfer the Black, Dwyfer the Black, welcome to my sacred space, sacred grove and sacred healing.' Witness a large black dragon entering your grove from all directions. Spend a few moments sitting in its energy…

Standing in the centre of your grove, it is time to meet Neptune, God of Ogam Healing. Speak the Intention, "My intention is to meet with Neptune, my intention is to meet with Neptune, my intention is to meet with Neptune."

As if from nowhere, Neptune appears before you in all his glory. You instantly feel a connection as your eyes lock with this great God...

Smiling he bestows a greeting upon you. You notice his trident; in time this will become a symbol to use to call him and access his energy. Take time to feel what it is like to have this God merge his energies with you. Neptune has a special message for you and gives it...

It is time to close the grove for now. We do this by giving thanks to the grove, the elements, your guardian, Neptune and anyone else that might have appeared to you during this time. Taking three deep breaths, we use our intention to make our way out of the grove gate, back down the path and into our physical bodies, in the physical world. Back into the room and the here and now. Once we know we are back, we rub our hands together, wriggle our toes, yawn, stretch, and open our eyes. Now make notes on your experiences.

Note: Neptune's symbol is the trident. Draw it within yourself, starting with the left-hand point moving down into 'u' shape curve from left shoulder and up to the right shoulder. Then from your head down to your feet, with the third point moving downwards into the shaft of the trident throughout your body.

Meditation Two: Meeting and Attuning with the Trees and their Deities

... (e.g Silver Birch)

Note: Before you journey to meet with our first tree, look at the notes and pictures later in this book, so you will recognise it in some form. Read of its uses, both in a physical sense and spiritual. Perhaps choose a healing you would like to experience. Then practice drawing the Ogam symbol of this tree. Do it physically and also in your mind's eye. Remember that you will be placing it in your crown, forehead, spirit gate, throat, heart chakras, as well as your palms and soles of the feet. Look also and choose which deity you wish to meet and work with today that is associated with this tree.

(Undertake the directions as above to enter your grove, meet with your guardian, call in the elements, bring in Neptune and tell them of your intention).

...ask your guardian to lead you to the path that will take you to the Silver Birch tree. Speak your intention, "My intention is to find the Silver Birch tree and attune myself with its energies, my intention is to find the Silver Birch tree and attune myself with its energies, my intention is to find the Silver Birch tree and attune myself with its energies..."

You may go alone or ask your guardian to guide you. It is up to you. You follow the path through the wood until drawn into a clearing where the Silver Birch is found. It is tall, magical and surrounded by a silvery light...

You ask for the spirit of the Silver Birch tree to make itself known to you...

See the spirit come out of the tree or know that it is time to approach the tree. You might hug it or sit with your back against the trunk. The spirit may lead you into the centre of the tree...

Once you are connected, draw the Silver Birch symbol in your head chakra... forehead chakra... spirit gate chakra... throat chakra... heart chakra... the palms of the hand... and the soles of your feet... You see and feel this tree filling you up with its energy...

Silver birch might have a message for you, spoken, visual, or symbolic...

You now ask for the healing you desire and experience it. As and when it is time to finish, Silver Birch will let you know...

It is time to meet one of the Gods and Goddesses that is linked with this tree. I call ... forth to meet with me here in the energy of the Silver Birch tree, I call ... forth to meet with me here in the energy of the Silver Birch tree, I call ... forth to meet with me here in the energy of the Silver Birch tree. Witness them appear before you. Ask them for a message, or a healing, or just spend some time in their energy...

Once they have indicated the meeting is at an end, ask them to accompany you back to your grove. They may follow or lead you back along the path to your grove. But before you go give thanks to the spirit of the tree...

Make your way back to the grove and take a few moments in the company of this deity, with Neptune, your guardian and any other ally that has appeared. Give thanks...

Now it is time to close the grove until next time. Taking three deep breaths, see and feel yourself leaving your grove via the gate, walking back down the pathway, coming fully back into your physical body and back into the room and the here and now. Once we know we are back, we rub our hands together, wriggle our toes, yawn, stretch, and open our eyes. Now make notes on your experiences.

Note: This meditation experience can be used for each tree in the Ogam list.

Meditation Three: Exploring the Grove

Before doing anything, create your intention, "My intention is to journey to my grove, meet my guardian and explore my grove."

Undertake the directions as above to enter your grove, meet with your guardian, call in the elements, bring in Neptune and tell them of your intention of exploring the immense wood of your grove...

Ask your guardian to lead you to the path that will lead you both into your wood and back out again. Speak your intention, "My intention is to explore the wood around my grove and come back safely once finished, my intention is to explore the wood of my grove and come back safely once finished, my intention is to explore the wood of my grove and come back safely once finished…"

You follow the path into the wood. It might be dark as in nighttime where you see the stars twinkling above you, or light as in daylight and see the sun sparking through the foliage above. Your senses start to come alive; you smell the scent of the trees and feel the pull of their energies…

You might hear the sound of small animals running about in the brush, the call of birds high above you, the sound of the running stream somewhere off in the distance. You might catch flashes of colour from these animals or other beings moving through the trees…

Every now and again, you hear the sound of song making its way to you, you wish to investigate where it's coming from and once you track it down, see a bright fire burning in a clearing with human figures dancing, singing and drumming in celebration about it...

If you are invited, you might join in, feeling the freedom that comes with movement and singing. An elder of this group comes to you in friendship and offers you a drink which you accept. It tastes of sweet nectar and a great feeling of peace and love fills you inside. You are welcome back at any time to meet with this group…

When the time is right you make your leave and now find yourself moving along the path, noticing the texture of the bark on the trees, the scent of their flowers, you might take a nut or berry if offered…

Now go where you will, knowing that it is safe to explore in this, your Ogam wood…

In time you know it is time to come back to the grove and so in this knowledge you may turn round and make your way back, or continue knowing that the path will return you safely to your grove…

Once back you discuss your experience with your guardian and Neptune and then, give your thanks.

Now it is time to close the grove until next time. Taking three deep breaths, see and feel yourself leaving your grove via the gate, walking back down the pathway, coming fully back into your physical body and back into the room and the here and now. Once we know we are back, we rub our hands together, wriggle our toes, yawn, stretch, and open our eyes. Now make notes on your experiences.

The Ogam Trees

There are many experiences to be had within your grove, don't try to do them all at once but visit as regularly as you can to build up your relationship with it, the trees, the land, creatures, and allies within. Once you have done this, you will have a magical, safe place to come for healing and advice.

6

Physical Healing Session

When working with a client, it is usual to have spoken with them about what is it they have come to you for. In other words, you will by now know what is it that needs healing and how you are going to go about this. Once they have disclosed what the illness, dis-ease or concern is, check in the tree chapters to see which tree healing covers it (in some cases you will have a choice). You might also want to check in with your Ogam guardian for help if it is not clear.

Get your client to sit or lie down and open your grove up if you have not already done this. You might have already prepared the room before your client arrives, cleansing and charging it with grove energy in readiness for their visit. The healing will work just as well if the client is either sitting or lying down.

Please note, choose only one tree energy to work with at any time, although you might also wish to use Neptune and or the deity related to the tree energy, or both to help within your healing session.

Meet with your guardian and give thanks for the healing today.

Call in the Elements.

Call in Neptune.

Create the intention of healing work you are about to undertake, 'I call in my Ogam healing grove and all the tree spirits within.' See them about you. 'I give thanks for the healing work we undertake today with *client's name* for the greatest and highest good of all concerned.'

Then carry out a diagnostic energy check on their body to see if you can see/feel what exactly needs doing. A client may not have given you all the details and there might be more than one thing that needs attention. There could be links from one part of the body to another which even they don't know about.

To do this, run your hands above their bodies (about four inches) starting around the head, then come down the throat, shoulders, chest, stomach, genitals, thighs, lower legs and feet.

Feel for any anomalies in the energy that might show up as pins and needles, hot or cold spots, vibrant or dead spots, they will make themselves known to you through your senses.

Have the intention that "This body in front of me is showing me what area needs healing." If you get a reaction, add it to your healing list.

You might also like to ask your guardian to show you where there is healing needed in the client's body. When looking at the client's body, it might come to your inner vision as darkness or in symbolic form as in something (an insect, animal, inanimate object, darkness, negative) that shouldn't be in the body.

Intention is everything in this work, whether you are a seer, feeler, hearer, sniffer etc… There are many ways of working with spiritual healing energy.

Calling in the Specific Tree Energy You Wish.

This can be done by going to the tree in your grove and tuning into the spirit of the tree, or by just calling out its name three times whilst tracing out its Ogam symbol in big form in front of you. Experiment and find what work best for you.

You might like to also re-trace the Ogam symbol mentally/physically into your chakras. Starting with your crown, third eye, spirit gate, throat, heart, palms and soles of the feet.

Take the time to feel the tree's energy come into you. Now tune into the specific part of this energy, e.g. heart healing energy from Huath and the Hawthorne tree. Feel the energy come down through your crown, visualise it, sense it pooling in your heart and then channel it from your heart into your hands and then place your hands on the part of the client's body you wish to work on. You might also like to draw the symbol over that part of the client's body.

Let the energy flow out your hands and into the client's body. Note: If in a delicate (sexual in nature) place; do not touch the body but work in the energy body which is roughly 2-4 inches above the physical body. Feel it go in, see it go in and work for as long as it feels right. Work around the area and any other places that were shown to you. You might like to channel the healing energy straight into the chakras related to that point in the body (see chakra section for details).

How long on each point?

Work on each part of the body for as long as you feel necessary. You might like to change the pattern of your hands, so you come from different angles. Go with your intuition, as one place gets the attention, another might show up as needing working on too (energy can move). If you have diagnosed there might be a number of spots that need work on, take your time and work through them all, one by one.

Keep the visualizing going throughout the work. You can chant the tree name, it's Ogam Irish name, visualize the deity you are working with, see yourself as the tree in question channelling through to your heart and from there, through your hands, into the client's body.

Positive Intent

If working on a client's stress and anxiety, call forth the tree energy (there will be options) for working with that intent but then channel the positivity needed to deal with that issue.

Beech: Peace and tranquillity.

Don't use words like *stress and anxiety* in your intent, but the positive energy that you want the patient to receive.

Power Song

In Shamanism, power songs are used to help channel the healing energy. Try to come up with a simple rhyme that uses the intent you want to achieve. You can sing/chant/intone/ dance/move as you do this.

For example, to channel Beech energy for stress and anxiety issues I have used the following:

'Channelling Beech Energy

Peace and tranquillity into thee.'

Power Words

Names/ words hold power.

Chant or sing the word Beech or its Ogam Irish name Eamhanchol.

Love is another positive word to use.

The names of the deities.

The Green Man/ Green Woman

They symbolise the cycle of life, death and re-birth. They also symbolise the Godhood and its relationship with the life force of the Goddess, the female expression of divinity. When working with the Green man/woman, I call them in and they stand either side of me, sometimes merge but always help channel divine nature energy.

When used in distant healing, I see/feel them as the Goddess energy in one hand and the God energy held above it in the other with the client held in-between.

Being the Tree

Imagine yourself as the specific tree you are channelling. Feel its energies come into your heart and out your hands/eyes/ intent...

Passing Energy into the Body

When channelling the energy, you might hold your hands on the desired area or just above it and let the healing energy move in on its own accord, or move your hand/hands in a circular clockwise direction which helps to screw the energy in. You can use your eyes to project the healing energy to where it needs to go, or even the tips of your fingers to get into specific points (there are minor chakra points here also).

Pulling Negative Energy out of the Body.

There will be times when you might wish to pull negative energy out of the client's body. See or feel this energy and pull it out by moving your hand/hands in a counter-clockwise direction knowing you are pulling it out as you go. Then return to channelling positive healing energy back into that part of the body.

Deposing of Negative Energy

You can use the intention of pulling it out and sending it to where it needs to go (all energy has its place of existence) and so it will go there, or you might wish to have a bowl of salted water beside you in the room to place it in and then flush down the loo or sink afterwards, intending it to go where it needs to go. It is enough to pull and flick towards the water with the intention of it entering and staying put, rather than placing your hands into the water each time. Once finished please do remember to physically wash your hands thoroughly whatever way you have used.

Grounding

Once you have worked on the diagnosed areas and their chakra related points to gain direct access to specific organs, you may feel drawn to balance the body by placing your hands first at one end of the body, i.e. head, and then down at the other, feet. See the body in front of you getting balanced and grounded.

Sealing the Healing

Seal the healing in at the end of the session by tracing the Ogam symbol above their body with the intent that the healing has taken place for the highest good of all concerned and is now safely placed within their body.

Time, as in Past, Present, Future

You may go back in time, heal in the present or set the healing to come to your client at whatever time you have agreed (when they are relaxed and ready to receive) later. Spirit works outside the confines of the third dimension so setting healing to be received at a specific time is a done thing. This is usually achieved in distant healing. The client should not take recreational drugs, alcohol etc for one day before, during or after the healing session, to let the healing settle in their bodies and take effect.

Medication

If your client is on any sort of on medication, tell them to always check with their doctor after a session as the medication might need to be changed due to the healing they have received.

Giving Thanks

Once you have finished, thank the tree for its energy, thank your allies/deities for their work and step away from the client.

Client After Care

When it is time to bring them back into the room (awake), ask them to... 'Please take three deep breaths and bring your consciousness back into the room.'

Have a glass of water ready for them but speak softly to them first of what just happened. Let them know the work has been done and any messages/ sacred prescriptions you might have been given for them. Offer the water, they do not have to take it.

Sacred Prescription

Spirit may well give you directions for your client to follow to help aid the healing settle into their systems. This might include walking in nature, meditating or undertaking a pilgrimage of some sort.

Client Feedback

When your client is ready, they might like to discuss the experience. Be aware of time, as sometimes they have had new experiences and may feel slightly dizzy. You can always agree to discuss things later. Ideally, clients should not get in a car straight after a session but be picked up by a friend.

Closing The Grove

Once your client has left the building and you have completed the work, remember to close your healing grove down and give a final word of thanks. Then sit in quiet contemplation of what you have completed. You may like to ask that any access healing energy left in the room go back into the universe.

Journal

When ready, write down your experiences.

Final Thing

Make sure you tidy up and wash your hands as a final act of self-cleansing.

Notes

There are numerous ways of approaching healing using the Ogam energy. One person on my workshops revealed that once they had they witnessed the tree cover the client and transferred its energies into them. Once the healing had been completed, the client gave back positive feedback. Sometimes it is easier to complete the work via distant healing, using a doll to represent the client (please see Distant Healing Section).

Probably the most important piece of advice from Neptune to me was to keep the intention short and to the point. Don't get caught up trying to remember three or four lines of waffle. What do you want? Ask that the healing be for the highest and greatest good of all concerned. You have the tools to succeed and change people's lives, including your own. Stand tall and know you are not working alone; this energy is ready and waiting to be used.

7

Distant Healing

As spirit works outside the three-dimensional world it can also work outside the timeframe, we live in. We can do a healing for someone and programme spirit to deliver it at a set time later that night or week if appropriate, or for even events in the past!

I regularly do divination work for people who have not thought up their question at the time of receiving my answer, but I send the answer anyway. Once they have thought of their question, they check out the answer. I have also completed healing in the afternoon as we could not find a time to suit us both and asked spirit to deliver the healing at a time when the client is in the right frame of mind to receive. It works, even if they are asleep.

I will open my grove and undergo all the steps as above before starting. In distant healing you won't have the clients sitting in front of you but normally will have had some contact. The sound of their voice over the phone, their name and address, or even a photo will help make a connection. When opening your grove, you will need to call them into the grove by name, address, or photo.

Once inside your grove, we usually have an object to represent them in front of us to work on. What do we use? In shamanic work, we go out into nature with the intention of finding a stick that represents the client. You will know when you find the right one.

In other energy-based healing work we use a doll or teddy bear to represent the client. It is important that you practise so that you find that which works best for you. I place the teddy in front of me and ask that the client's physical, etheric, emotional, mental and spiritual bodies be represented in this teddy. I ask for it, I see it, I know it. It is done.

There are times when I use none of the above but can bring the client's *spiritual* body into the room and within my healing grove. This way, you can rise them up to a comfortable level to work on without having to bend too low down. It is the intention that counts. You might also shrink them down and hold them between your hands.

For a distant healing to have most benefit, a time for the healing will have to be arranged when the client is in a relaxed place of being. It is ok if they fall asleep, it is ok if they feel everything you undertake, and it is ok if they feel nothing. You are doing the work with spirit and spirit does not lie. Once the work has been completed, it is usual for spirit to tell you, "The work has been done," or you will just know.

When finishing with the distant work, you must not use the stick again for anyone else's healing. Take the doll or teddy and cleanse it spiritually by holding it in one hand and passing your other hand over and around it, from top to bottom with the intention of cleansing it of the client's energies and any residue that might have remained. Then go and wash your hands, asking for any remaining positive healing energy to go into the universe.

Resistance to Healing

There will be times when you feel that the energy you are channelling is being repulsed or pushed back. When this happens, do not panic! There are times when the negative energy which might have been building for many years, takes time to break down before being removed.

Sometimes the client is undergoing an experience through their dis-ease/illness which is for their highest good and it would not be right to interfere in their journey.

You might meet a client who doesn't believe in this type of healing or are adamant that they deserve the illness that they are experiencing and so self-block any attempts by others to help them. So be it. You can lead a horse to water, but they won't always drink. Nowadays if a potential client is particularly obstinate or tries to challenge me, I won't waste my time by working with them. They are welcome to their beliefs, but if they are willing to give it a go, so am I.

8

The Twelve Hand Positions for Self-Healing and Healing Others

The following are the standard traditional hand positions for energy healing. By using these positions, you will hit all major glands, body parts and organs. If you find it difficult to reach your own back, use your intention to send the energy from the front of the body to the needed areas in the spine or back.

You can also apply this reasoning when working with a client. Ogam energy will enter the chakra system at the front and travel to the back, or vice-versa. The two hands are usually placed beside each other, so that the thumbs are just touching and lowered gently down to either rest upon the client's body or hover just above it. Be sensitive to the area of body you are working on and always ask if your client is prepared for you to touch them or would rather not. It doesn't matter whether you touch or not as you will be working within their energy body and so the healing will connect with their physical body always.

The Head

Top of Head (Crown)

Full on face: (Eyes, forehead, mouth)

Sides of Head (Temples)

Back of Head (Occipital region)

Front of neck (Throat)

Front of Body

Above the Chest (Heart Chakra)

Below Chest (Solar Plexus Chakra)

Either Side of the Navel (Abdomen) (Navel Chakra)

Below Navel (Pelvic Region - Groin) (Base Chakra)

Back

Shoulders (Top of Shoulders)

High up on Rib Cage (Shoulder Blades – Beam from the front)

Lower Back (Kidneys)

Base of Spine (Tail Bone)

Extras

Arms

Shoulders

Elbows

Wrists

Hands

Legs

Hips

Thighs

Knees

Lower legs

Ankles

Feet

Not Able to Reach a Particular Hand Position?

Energy can be sent from one side of the body to the other. It can be sent up to the head, or down to the legs or feet. Ogam energy runs through you and exits from your hands, heart, or eyes. Use your intention. By connecting your personal energy meridians (see below) you will enable a smoother and greater flow of energy. You do not want to lose any through major points of escape.

Two Main Acupuncture Meridians

The Central Channel runs from the mouth (under the back of the tongue) down the middle front of the body, to the perineum (which is between the anus and the genitals). The Governing channel runs from the perineum up the middle back of the body, over the top of the head and finishes up on the top lip.

The Mouth

The two meridians mentioned above do not automatically connect in the mouth as there is a large hole from the mouth extending deep down into the body. Therefore, when Ogam energy is brought down through the crown chakra and channelled into the hands, there is the possibility for the energy to escape into or out of the mouth on the in or out breath. To prevent it escaping simply connect the two meridians by gently touching the tip of your tongue against the gum above the teeth, just inside the top of the mouth.

The Hui Yin

The hui yin (Reiki term) is found by the perineum which sits between the anus, the genitals and the base chakra. The hui yin point is in a muscle that is usually weak and underused. Take the time to exercise it by contracting it. Some healers have found that they have lost healing energy from that point instead of feeling it in their hands.

Developing the Hui Yin

Contract the area/muscle between the anus and genitals about 30 times a time.

When to Connect Both Mouth and Hui Yin

There will be times when it is not necessary to connect the meridians because the Ogam energy will be seemingly flowing in a positive relevant way. Practice channelling and then placing your tongue into position and contracting the hui yin area and see if you can feel a difference.

Using the Chakras

Connect the client's chakra to the part of the body you wish to work on. For example, heart chakra for the heart and Hawthorn energy.

9

Drawing the Symbols

The energy associated with each symbol can be unlocked and channelled from the inner worlds into you by drawing it in a correct sequence of moves. This technique came to me one day as I was in meditation sitting with my oak tree. I had asked for it to channel some of its energy to help with my inner spiritual development when the spirit of the tree told me to use the Ogam symbol. I drew the oak symbol and suddenly felt an increase of energy. The spirit of the oak referred me to my past energy healing training and revealed that the process was similar.

So, for the next month, I journeyed to a new tree in my Ogam grove every day and sat in meditation with its spirit. They showed me how to draw their symbols and place in my chakras. I was also told that I could access this energy by sitting beside the tree in the physical world and draw its symbol. The energy is there waiting to be used.

I was also informed that it was beneficial for us to make a relationship with each tree in the inner world as well as the outer worlds. The stronger your links, the easier to access its energy. I spent many months, visiting each tree in turn, channelling, talking and soaking up as much information as I could to write this book. The process is ongoing, as the original reason for getting interested in Ogam was because of its divination use. I have also been working with the Ogam trees for meditation and magic work. I have no doubt that there is a wealth of other uses Ogam can be applied, so far unearthed. The Ivy tree/plant appeared first thing in the morning one day, in a vision, to remind me that whilst I was channelling the specific tree energy, I should also see myself as this tree.

Look at each tree section in turn and practice drawing the symbol using the guide given. Do it in your mind's eye and also with your forefinger. Then go to the chapter which tells you how to create your inner Ogam grove. Meet with the tree and attune yourself to its energy as shown. Keep a notebook to record your experiences.

I have also included Mistletoe with the Heather symbol in the fourth aicme. I found this in Liz and Colin Murray's book Celtic Tree Oracle. I liked the fact we can get two themes out of the one symbol and gives us more opportunity for healing.

10

The Ogam Trees

Code

Deciduous: This type of tree sheds its leaves annually.

Evergreen: This type of tree retains it leaves throughout the year.

Conifer: This type of tree bears cones and needle-like or scale-like leaves that are typically evergreen.

Perennial: Lives more than two years

Dioecious: This type of tree has its male and female reproductive organs in separate trees.

Monoecious: This type of tree has its male and female reproductive organs in the same tree.

Pronunciation

Pronunciation of the Irish Ogam tree name will change with the many different dialects that range from around Ireland and also whether you are using old Irish or modern Irish. I suggest you find a way of making it sound authentic to yourself and go with the intention of connecting with the energy behind the sound to make it work. When chanting or intoning the word, take it slowly and you will find that a pronunciation will come to you. Modern thought on the word Ogam, is to pronounce it with a silent G.

Birch   Beith   (Birth)

Beith corresponds to the letter B in the Ogam alphabet and is associated with the Silver Birch tree. This symbol represents new beginning, change, purity and rebirth.

Beith: Pronounced Beyh

Status: Peasant-tree

Element: Water

Gender: Feminine

Celtic First Month: November

Powers: Beith is the beginning of a new year is an opportunity to start with a clean slate.

Keywords

Beginnings, change, purity, protection, cleansing, foundation and vitality. It affects both the physical and the spiritual realms.

Deities associated with Birch

Thor, Frigga, Eostre, Lugh, Freya.

Tree Description

The Silver birch tree is native to Europe and parts of Asia. It is a hardy deciduous tree, which usually grows to between 20-30m, is fast growing, but rarely lasts more than 100 years. It starts out as a conical tree but can distort outwards and prefers dry, sandy, peaty soils though can often be found on moorland. It is seen as a *pioneer species* as it often appears as the first tree on empty or fire-swept land.

The bark is golden-brown at first, later turning to white. A papery tissue develops on the surface which then peels off in flakes. The bark stays smooth until the tree gets larger, but as it ages, it thickens, becomes irregular, dark and rugged. Young branches have whitish resin warts, and the twigs are slender, hairless and often pendulous, drooping down from the stiffer branches.

The species has both male and female catkins found in the same tree. Its leaves are oval with a long-pointed tip, the edges are toothed, but with smaller teeth in between the teeth formed by the main veins. The foliage is a pale to medium green and turns yellow early in the autumn before falling. In mid-summer, the female catkins mature, and the male catkins expand and release pollen, and wind pollination takes place. The small 1 to 2 mm winged seeds ripen in late summer and fall in the autumn.

Uses

Silver birch is often planted in parks and gardens, grown for its white bark and gracefully drooping shoots. In Scandinavia and other regions of northern Europe, it is grown for forest products such as lumber and pulp, as well as for aesthetic purposes and ecosystem services.

It is sometimes deliberately used as a pioneer and nurse tree.

Silver birch wood is pale in colour with no distinct heartwood and is used in making furniture, plywood, veneers, parquet blocks, skis, kitchen-utensils and in turnery. It makes a good firewood that produces a good heat but burns quickly. Thin sheets of bark peeled off young trees contain a waxy resin which is easy to ignite even when wet. The dead twigs are also useful as kindling for outdoor fires. Slabs of bark are used for making roof shingles and strips are used for handicrafts such as wooden footwear and small containers. Historically, the bark was used for tanning. Bark can be heated, and the resin collected; the resin is an excellent waterproof glue and useful for starting fires.

In the spring, the sap rises up the trunk and can be tapped. It contains around 1% sugars and can be used in a similar way to maple syrup. It can be drunk fresh, concentrated by evaporation and even fermented into a wine. In Sweden, the bark was ground up and used to make famine food as in bark bread. Also, in Sweden and Lapland, birch sap replaces sugar.

Criminals used to be *birched* to help drive out the negative influences in them. Native Americans used birch bark in the making of canoes, ribbed with cedar and bound with larch roots. Pine resin would be used to make its seams watertight.

Interesting Spiritual Information

Birch has been associated with fertility, healing, new beginnings, purification, protection, creativity and birth. Its twigs are used as wands/rods to bestow fertility onto cattle and newlyweds, cradles were made from its wood. Birch wood bark has been used in love spells.

Tree Medicine

The silver birch has long been used in traditional medicine for a wide range of ailments, including inflammatory conditions, urinary tract disorders, psoriasis and eczema. Oil extracted from its bark contains methyl salicylate, and decoctions were traditionally used for their anti-inflammatory effects in both arthritis and gout, and oil of wintergreen is produced from birch tar.

In Russia, the buds were traditionally preserved in spirit (vodka) and used as a treatment for many inflammatory conditions. Because of the presence of salicylates, products containing birch extracts are contraindicated in those people who are sensitive to aspirin. Its buds can also be eaten to stimulate digestion.

The leaves contain flavonoids, which have a diuretic action, but certain studies show that diuresis might not be due to just the flavonoids, the high potassium content of the leaves may also contribute. The birch acts as an effective germicide. Water from its leaves or trunk can be used to break up kidney and bladder stones.

It makes a good mouthwash, the bark produces xylitol, a chemical which inhibits the growth of major decay forming bacteria. The inner bark can be used as a pain reliever. Its leaves can be used to treat arthritis.

Also present in the bark are other triterpene substances which have been shown to have anti-inflammatory, antiviral and anti-cancer properties. Recent research has focused on betulinol, which is a compound found in the bark of the tree. Tests have shown betulinic acid, synthesized from betulinol, inhibits division of human prostate cancer cells implanted into mice, and may even facilitate the death of those cells.

Silver birch is reputed to be useful in the treatment of high blood pressure, high cholesterol, obesity, gout, kidney stones, nephritis, cystitis, digestive disturbances and respiratory diseases. Birches can lower the body temperature, eliminate body moisture and help to detoxify the body. To help increase immunity of the body, collect a bundle of birch leaves and place in a bag in your bedroom. Before you go to sleep open the bag and leave it open overnight. In the morning, close the bag so the energy of the day does not disturb them.

A birch in the garden helps to protect the microbial area. It has been demonstrated in times of cholera epidemics or plague, when houses with birches in were allegedly bypassed by the tainted molluscs.

Herbal Medicine: Betula pendula

Common Name: Birch, silver birch.

Parts used: Bark, leaf buds, leaves, sap (tapped from the trunk).

Overview: Birch tar is made from the bark. However, the main medicinal parts of the tree are the leaves, either gathered in bud or when fully opened. They are diuretic and anti-inflammatory, providing positive benefits in joint diseases (such as arthritis and gout) by decreasing the levels of uric acid in the body. Birch can also be taken internally for bladder disorders (such as cystitis and kidney stones) and rheumatism (muscular pain). Birch wine can be made from the sap when taken from the trunk of the tree.

Juice: Juice pressed from the fresh leaves, taken at 10ml twice a day in water.

Sap: Taken fresh or preserved with alcohol as a diuretic and anti-flammatory.

Tea: Infusion of the leaves, taken 3 to 4 times a day. The tea is aromatic and refreshing.

Ointment: An ointment is made with birch tar oil and applied externally to psoriasis and eczema; patches created as required.

Cautions: None found.

Ogam Channel Healing Guide

Spiritual/ Mind: Change (Regenerate yourself)   Cleansing   Depression   Diet foundation and vitality   Free creative imagination   Help in diets   New beginnings   Obesity   Protection   Seeing the bigger picture   Strengthening will   Protecting mothers and their young   Purity

Head/Neck: Teeth/ mouthwash

Chest/Heart: Antiviral illnesses   Cholesterol levels   Detoxing the body   High blood pressure   Respiratory diseases

Stomach: Digestion/ Diuretic   Obesity

Kidney/Urinary: Cystitis   Kidney and bladder disorders   Kidney and bladder stones   Urinary tract disorders   Nephritis

Skin: Pain reliever for inflammations   Infections of the skin such as eczema and psoriasis

Joints: Rheumatism   Arthritis   Anti-inflammatory   Gout

Cancer: Prostate cancer

General: Body de-tox

Flower Remedy

Birch flower remedy opens your mind and helps to broaden your outlook on life, gets rid of uncertainty and worry. Helps you to see the bigger picture. The essence can aid you in opening the door to your mind, to help free your creative imagination and see things afresh from different angles. From there it is a much easier route to your envisioned goals.

Notes

The birch acts as a doorway to the Underworld as it is a tree of the Fey and known as the Lady of the Woods. The silver birch is feminine, constant and friendly, a tree of enchantment. When coming into your life it represents the opportunity to start a new quest, an adventure that will prove to be the unfolding of your destiny.

Folklore

In Celtic cultures, the birch symbolized growth, renewal,

stability, initiation and adaptability because its ability to sustain harsh conditions. In the Gaelic creation myth, Dagda, the god of Nature, played creation into being using a harp made from birch. The music encouraged the seasons to wax and wane and so the cycle of life began.

Birch is dedicated to the Norse goddess Frigga, goddess of married love, the sky and clouds, she became Odin's wife. She had eleven hand maidens who helped in the caring for humanity and so she spins golden threads and the rainbows of spring. It is said that her seven mortal sons founded the seven Saxon kingdoms of England.

Ancient Finnish folklore has been set into traditional ballads and one of these is called the Kalevala. The hero, Vainamoinen, has many magic adventures as he travels through the ages of man to find a sacred talisman called the *Sampo*. When he loses his harp in a lake, he creates a new one from a sad and weeping birch. It is through this act he enabled the birch tree to bring great joy to the world with its music. Listening to this music freed all of nature to rejoice in the birches new expression and beautified the world.

In Scandinavian legend the birch was regarded to be the tree around which the last battle for worldly existence would be fought.

It is usually the first tree to repopulate areas damaged by forest fires or clearings, so it is no great surprise to see that birches are also associated with the land of the dead and the *Sidhe* in Gaelic folklore. They also appear in Scottish, Irish, and English folksongs and ballads in association with death, fairies, or returning from the grave. Birch garlands were given as tokens of love and birch wands used in love magic. The birch maypole was used in themes of fertility and regeneration celebrations.

Prisoners were often *birched* in a bid to free them from evil influences and in doing so emphasised the tree's purifying qualities. It was also seen as having the ability to drive out negative or evil spirits of the old year and was used in beating the bounds of a village. Birch rods were also used to beat out spirits and demons of the mad.

The birch is also believed by some to grow at the gates of paradise. It is primarily a tree of sun and sky. When first used in Ireland as the first Ogam tree inscription, it became associated with the sun-god Lugh, as this first inscription informed him that the Fey had captured his wife and taken her to their land.

Rowan   Luis   (Protection)

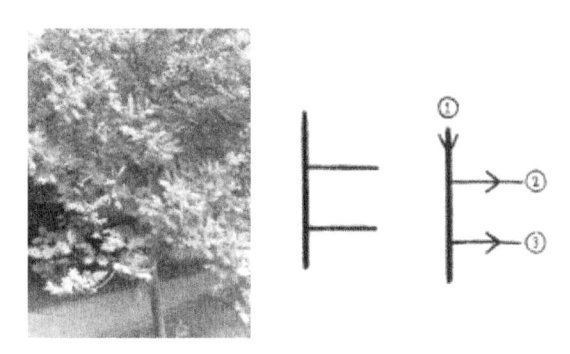

Luis corresponds to the letter L in the Ogam alphabet and is associated with the Rowan tree. The symbol represents protection, insight and control

Luis: Pronounced Loos

Status: Shrub

Element: Fire

Gender: Changeable

Celtic Second Month: December

Magical protection from harm and enchantment and helping keep control of all your senses.

Keywords

Tree of life, protection, nurturing, insight, control.

Deities associated with Rowan

Thor, Brighid.

Tree Description

The rowans or mountain-ashes (as they are also known), are native throughout the cooler regions of Europe, especially to the north and mountainous regions, where they grow higher than other deciduous trees. Usually, Rowans are found to be mostly small, slender trees, 10–20m tall, though a few are shrubs. Usually found on infertile soils, but where there is much rain.

The bark is smooth, shining, and grey-brown when it gets older. Rowans leaves are pinnate with usually 6-7 pairs of leaflets with a terminal leaflet always present. The flowers are creamy white, produced in May and are less than 10-15cm across, but where the dense flat-topped heads are found, can be larger. Its fruits are soft and juicy, almost spherical in shape, 6-9mm and bright scarlet by August.

Uses

Rowans are used as ornamental trees in gardens, parks and wildlife areas. In Finland, its wood has been used for horse sled shafts and rake spikes. The dense wood is used for carving and turning, specifically for tool handles and walking sticks. Rowan fruit is a traditional source of tannins for mordanting vegetable dyes. It can also be made into a slightly bitter jelly, eaten with game, made into preserves, or with other fruit. It can also be a substitute for coffee beans, and has many uses in alcoholic beverages, as flavored liqueurs, cordials in country wine, and flavored ales. It is very attractive to fruit-eating birds, which is reflected in the old name *bird catcher*.

Interesting Spiritual Information

The Rowan gives protection against magical enchantment. It helps in the control of your senses and in using your spiritual ability to repel anything that threatens your serenity or purpose. It has associations with divination, astral work, strength, protection, initiation, healing, psychic energies, working with the dead (spirits), personal power and success.

Runes were often carved on Rowan sticks. Sprays of Rowan were placed over cattle pens and doorways into the homes as a way of protection. The berries have a pentagram on them but may be poisonous if eaten raw. This is a symbol of protection and a sacred tree for Druids in particular. It protects and controls the senses from enchantment. A magical tree used by those who use magic in wands rods, amulets and spells.

Tree Medicine

Rowan competes with carrots for beta carotene content – both have about 9mg per 100g. They are also rich in vitamin c and contains also vitamin p, vitamin k, organic acids, sugars, pectins, flavonoids, tannins and essential oils. Its sugars contain mostly sorbose and from microelements manganese, iron, copper and also phosphorous and silicon. Rowan berries also have active agents, that act against microbes and bacteria, which means they preserve well and help other foods to slow down the fermentation.

Rowan berries are great for hypertension, kidney stones, flatulence, atherosclerosis, stomach hypoacidity and lymph gland infection. Pectin and tannins in rowan stop the fermentation of carbohydrates. Rowan berries have been found to be one of the strongest benders of toxic substances created in the intestines and helps restore normal microflora. The sorbose found in rowan improves bile discharge and lowers cholesterol.

It's a slight laxative, especially if the reason for constipation are biliary diseases.

Ascorbic acid is a very important element in human health, as it can stimulate the production of white blood cells and can also act as an antioxidant as well. Vitamin C is essential for a number of bodily processes, including the creation of collagen, which strengthens muscle tissue and helps build and repair blood vessels.

The fiber found in rowan berries, helps digestion and reduce constipation by building up the stool and optimizing your gastrointestinal system. In traditional medicine, rowan berry juice was used to reduce inflammation of the respiratory tract, improve sore throats and help relieve asthma and congestion. Finally, folk medicine readily recommends rowan berries for any kind of stones (kidney, bile, bladder), to help strengthen blood, and for respiratory disease and rheumatism.

Herbal Medicine: Sorbus Aucuparia

Common name: Rowan.

Parts Used: Bark, fruit.

Overview: The berries are stewed (usually with sugar, or apples) to make jellies and sauces and also used in making beer and spirits. The berries are high in vitamin C and good for sore throats and tonsillitis. Because of their astringent properties, both the berries and the bark have been used as a treatment for diarrhoea and sore throats.

Take 1 teaspoon of fresh berry juice or a quarter cup of the tea made by simmering 1 teaspoon per cup of water for 20 mins.

The bark is decocted for diarrhoea and for vaginal douches; simmer 2 teaspoons of bark per cup for 20 mins.

The bark is tinctured in alcohol for 8 days to treat fevers.

In Native American medicine the Potawatomi used the leaves to make tea to treat colds.

Cautions: Rowan berries contain parasorbic acid which are poisonous in their raw state. Once cooked, they become digestible due to the parasorbic acid being converted into sorbic acid which is harmless.

Ogam Channel Healing Guide

Spiritual/Mind: Accepting painful behaviours   Balance   Creating inner peace   Fear-based emotions   Mental-health issues   Nervousness   Personal power   PTSD   Psychic protection   Vision work   Moving on from traumas by taking responsibility for healing them

Head/Neck: Sore throats and inflamed tonsils   Eyes   Fevers

Heart: Cholesterol

Chest: Asthma   Bronchitis   Pneumonia   Hypertension

Lymph Glands: Immune system strengthening   Lymph gland infection

Stomach: Constipation   Diarrhoea   Digestive issues   Diuretic   Gall-bladder (inflammation, stones)   Stomach-complaints   Flatulence

Liver: Liver cirrhosis   Liver problems

Kidney: Kidney stones

Genital: Vaginal issues

Bowels: Haemorrhoids

Skin: Skin issues

Muscle: Muscle tissue

Joints: Rheumatism

General: Radiation and x-ray damage   Scurvy

Flower Remedy

Rowan flower essence helps you to move on from past traumas by taking personal responsibility for healing them and creating peace within yourself and others. The essence helps you accept responsibility for painful behaviour and actions. If negative emotions are not resolved they can easily manifest again in future situations and relationships which have nothing to do with the original trauma. You might well have to travel into the past to process these events, learn from the experience and then make amends.

Notes

The Rowen grows white flowers and red berries which are the colours of the Fey. This signifies that this is a magic tree with affiliations to witchcraft. Dowsing rods were commonly made from twigs as witch-wands. It has clear visionary qualities to help working in the astral or dream states. It also is known to feed the soul.

Folklore

The European rowan has a long tradition in European mythology and folklore as a magical tree which gives protection against evil things, especially witches. The tree was also called *wayfarer's tree* or *traveller's tree* because it apparently prevents people getting lost on journeys. In England this was also the tree on which the Devil hanged his mother.

If bird's droppings containing rowan seeds land in a space where old leaves have gathered on a larger tree, it may result in a rowan growing as an epiphyte on the larger tree. Such a rowan is called a *flying rowan* and was thought of as especially potent as a countercharm against sorcery and black magic. Rowan can also serve as protection against fairies by placing a rowan branch over your door.

In Norse mythology, the rowan is called *the salvation of Thor* because Thor once clung to it, saving himself from being swept to his death in a fast-flowing river below.

It is associated to both the lunar and solar cycles to pagans, who saw the red berries every month and at each quarter of the year. It staved off hunger month by month, was a healing plant which added a year to people's lives.

In Neo-Druidism, the rowan is known as the *portal tree*, marking the point between this world and the Underworld. It was often placed at the gate to a property, signifying the crossing of the threshold between the path or street and the property. The Old English name of the rowan is *cwic-beám*, which survives in the name quick beam. By the 19th century this name was reinterpreted as connected to the word *witch* and so is known by a number of names such as wicken tree, wich tree, wicky tree, wiggan tree, witch hazel and witch tree.

According to Greek legend it was regarded as the tree of life. The birth of this tree came about when the daughter of Zeus, Hebe, lost her mother's cup of the Gods when it was stolen by demons. The gods sent an eagle to recover it and deal with the demons, a battle ensued and wherever an eagle's feather or drop of blood fell to earth, there grew a rowan tree.

Rowan is under the planetary influence of the sun and strongly associated with two particular sun-goddesses, Brigid of Ireland and Brigantia of England. They both were the heads of river and water cults, protecting pastoral people and their animals. They were associated with spring and with it the season of birth.

Alder   Fearn   (Guidance)

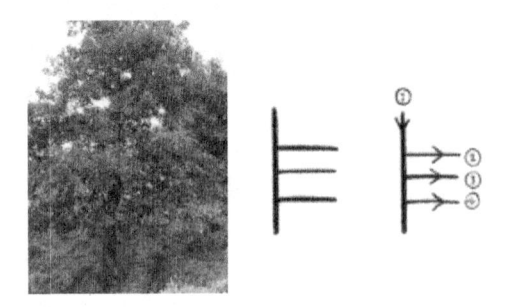

Fearn corresponds to the letter F or V in the Ogam alphabet and is associated with the Alder tree. This symbol represents strong spiritual foundation and principles, it also is linked with oracular powers.

Fearn pronounced: Fyarn

Status: Chieftain-tree

Element: Air, Fire, Water and Earth

Gender: Masculine

Celtic Third Month: January

Powers: Fearn gives good counsel and oracular power, combined with protection and strength.

Keywords

Divination, oracular powers, guidance, protection.

Deities associated with Alder

Bran, Apollo, Odin, King Arthur, Circe, Calypso.

Tree Description

Alder can be found throughout northern Europe and usually near streams, rivers, and wetlands. It rarely reaches higher than 20m but has reached 40m when cultivated. When young, its shape is unusually conical for a non-conifer, but once mature, grows open straggly crowns. Its bark is grey or brown, with a fine network of shallow fissures running through it.

Almost all alders are deciduous, the leaves are alternate and serrated. They are rounded, similar to hazel and often have an indented tip. They are bright green and shiny with 4-7 pairs of veins. The flowers are catkins. The male catkins are elongated and similar to birches, its colours contrast purple scale with yellow flowers and are on the same trees as the shorter female catkins (these distinguish Alder from similar trees by being cone-like in appearance) which remain on the trees after the seeds have shed.

Uses

The catkins of some alder species can be eaten because they are rich in protein. Although having a bitter and unpleasant taste, they can be used as famine food. The wood of certain alder species is used to smoke food items such as coffee, salmon and other seafood.

Its wood has been used as underwater foundations and pilings, as in piers, houses as in Venice etc... The inner bark of the alder, as well as red osier dogwood, or chokecherry, is used by some Native Indians from North America in smoking mixtures, known as *kinnikinnick*, to improve the taste of the bearberry leaf.

Since the 1950s, Fender guitars have been built with alder bodies as its wood is appreciated for its tight and even balanced tone. As a hardwood, alder is used in making furniture, cabinets, and other woodworking products. Alder bark and wood (like oak and sweet chestnut) contain tannin and are traditionally used to tan leather. A red dye can also be extracted from the outer bark, and a yellow dye from the inner bark.

Interesting Spiritual Information

The alder was sacred to the Druids and offers spiritual protection in arguments and the opportunity to use as an oracle. It is also associated with Bran, who used his body to as a bridge to span dangerous water ways. Bran's head was oracular. The wood has been used in bridge construction. There was a custom to use the alder as a whistle to entice air elements, and so the term *whistling up the wind* was born.

Tree Medicine

Reduces swellings, good for sore throats, mouth ulcers, bleeding gums and tonsillitis. Bags filled with heated alder leaves help with chronic skin diseases (skin conditions, eczema etc), inflamed and burnt skin. It can even help with haemorrhoids. Alder bark contains the anti-inflammatory salicin, which is metabolized into salicylic acid in the body. Alder oil and essence can help relieve stiffness in the muscles.

Ogam Channel Healing Guide

Spiritual/Mind: Divination   Negative attitudes   Oracular Guidance   Protection   Strength   Clarifying our perception of life at that moment in time on all levels

Head/Neck: Sore throats

Skin: Eczema   Skin irritations   Burns

Bowels: Haemorrhoids

Muscles: Stiff muscles

General: Swellings

Flower Remedy

Alder flower remedy helps us when we cannot see the deeper meaning of the lessons we are receiving in life. When we are unable to see what we sense or know is true and taking life at face value. It can help clarify perception on all levels so that we can both see and know our highest truth at that moment in time.

Notes

The alder tree brings you the gifts of prophecy and the creative arts which stem from the Underworld of the Fey. With these gifts from the tree, you have the ability to explore the world in your distinct way, using your intuition.

Folklore

The alder has special implications in Celtic tradition as it is especially associated with Bran, at Cad Goddeu, *The Battle of the Trees*. Gwydion guessed Bran's name from the alder twigs in his hand. The answer to an old Taliesin riddle, *why is the Alder purple?* is, 'Because Bran wore purple.' Bran's alder may be a symbol of resurrection. Bran's shamanistic birds were ravens who acted as scouts and messengers for him. When his head was buried under the White Hill, his ravens stayed to guard him, and carry out any desires he might have. To this day, the ravens at the Tower of London are well guarded as it is said that should they ever leave the tower, Britain will fall.

The name for the boy Gwern, son of Matholwch and Branwen, means *alder*. In Ireland the alder was regarded with awe as when cut the wood turns from white to red. At one time the cutting down of an alder tree was punishable, and it is still avoided today.

The alder was thought to have power of divination, especially in the diagnosing of diseases. Alder was used as a fe, a rod for measuring corpses and graves in pre-Christian Ireland. In Irish legend the first man was formed from an alder, the first woman was made from a rowan.

In ancient Greece, Cronos was represented by the alder tree. One of his epithets was *faerinus*, now translated as meaning 'of the dawn of the year, as in springtime when plant life starts to grow.

In Norse legends, March was known as 'the lengthening month of the waking alder.' This time was called *Lenct*, a period of fasting as their supplies ran low. It was adopted by the Church which renamed this time as Lent. In Italy, alder is associated with springtime fire festivals.

Willow   Saille   Intuition

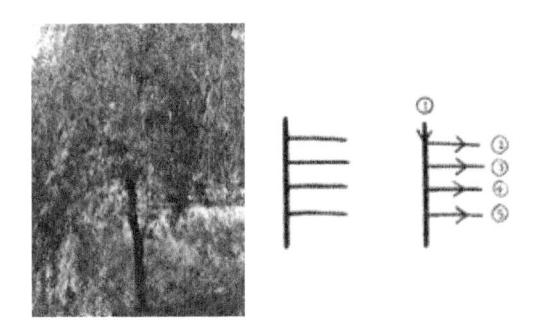

Saille corresponds to the letter S in the Ogam alphabet and is associated with the Willow tree. The symbol represents spiritual growth and knowledge wisely applied. A strong feminine influence bringing you healing and protection.

Saille pronounced: SOL-yeh

Status: Peasant-tree

Element: Water

Gender: Feminine

Celtic Fourth Month: February

Powers: Saille brings creativity, clairvoyance, dreaming visions and is linked with feminine aspects.

Keywords

Clairvoyance, dreaming visions, divination, lunar cycles, rhythm, femininity, fertility, inspiration, seership, magic, positive hidden influences.

Deities associated with Willow

Persephone, Circe, Hecate, Hera, Belili, Artemis, Selene, Diana, Luna, Athena, Cerridwen, Helice, Ceres. Orpheus, Bel, Belin, Mercury, Jehovah.

Tree Description

Weeping Willows are found usually on moist soils in cold and mild regions of the Northern hemisphere. Willows have an abundant watery bark sap, which is full of salicylic acid. The wood is soft, pliant and tough, but have thin branches and large roots. The leaves are elongated but may also be round to oval with serrated edges and come in a great variety of greens, ranging from yellowish to a bluish colour. Willows have male and female flowers appearing as catkins on separate plants; these are produced in early spring, before the leaves. Willows are often planted to protect the bank against the rivers and streams beside them. Their interlacing roots help keep the banks solid and sometimes you will find that the roots are much larger than the trunk they grow from.

Uses

In the past, the willow was used for making fishing nets, baskets, fish traps, wattle fences, wattle and daub house walls. The old Welsh coracle boat traditionally used willow in the framework. Willow wood is used in the manufacture of furniture, including boxes, cricket bats and brooms. They are also used in flutes, poles, turnery tool handles, veneer, wands and whistles. Tannin, fibre, paper, rope and string can also be produced from the wood.

Willow has been used in the making of musical double bass instruments. Bees can make honey from the little amount of nectar that the willow produces, and it is especially valued as a source of early pollen for them too. Poor people at one time ate cooked willow catkins as a mash (another form of famine food). Willow is used to make drawing charcoal and in living sculptures, which are live willow rods planted in the ground and woven into interesting shapes, including domes and tunnels. Willow stems are also used to create garden features, such as decorative panels and obelisks.

Interesting Spiritual Information

The willow stands for female and lunar rhythms of life. The gift of fertility is strong here, as are also the gifts of seership and dream visions. Balance is sought with the male energies. The catkins which appear before the leaves, attract bees to start the act of pollination. Willow indicates cycles, rhythms and the ebb and flux. It is a Moon tree sacred to the White Lady.

When in a willow grove, Druid priests and priestesses would use it for inspiration, hone their skills, ask for prophecies and gain eloquence. It is a good tree to ask a wish from. It has long been considered a special tree due to its protection qualities against negative entities and used in many rituals. Broken willow branches continue to emit their own positive energy until it has completely dried and lost all leaves.

Tree Medicine

Willow acts as a painkiller and is used in treatment of fevers, colds, headache, and neuralgia. It lowers the blood pressure in the small capillaries and blood vessels in the head, so helping to combat migraines and easing pressure. It can also be applied externally to wounds. The leaves and bark of the willow tree have been mentioned in ancient texts from Assyria, Sumer and

Egypt as a remedy for aches and fever. It has a rich blend of antioxidants and organic compounds. For thousands of years, it has been traditionally used to relieve pain from injuries and illness with great success and was used in Chinese traditional medicine more than 2,500 years ago.

Tea made from its bark is used to treat fevers, rheumatism, coughs and other inflammatory conditions. It can help eliminate inflammation in the respiratory tracts, gastrointestinal system and joints. If the bark is used as a tea it can help with arthritis, irritable bowel syndrome and gout. Willow bark helps in the reduction of fevers and speed up the healing process aiding the organs back into good health.

It can help with women's heavy periods or severe menstrual symptoms, cramps and mood swings. It rebalances the hormones in a woman's body.

The willows help to eliminate excess moisture from the body, reducing blood pressure and strengthen the urinary tract and bladder. In Ancient Greece the physician Hippocrates wrote about its medicinal properties. Native Americans relied on it as a staple of their medical treatments. It provides temporary pain relief. Salicin is metabolized into salicydic acid in the human body and is a precursor of aspirin. This has given rise to the important class of drugs known as nonsteroidal anti-inflammatory drugs (NSAIDs).

The high tannin content soothes the stomach and can prevent gastrointestinal distress when your immune system is weak. The high content of antioxidant compounds can have a big impact on the health of the skin, by increasing the blood flow to it and reducing the appearance of wrinkles and ease the pain of insect bites.

Herbal Medicine: Salix alba

Common Name: White willow

Parts used: Bark

Overview: Willow contains salicin which is converted by the digestive metabolism into salicylic acid and creates willow's anti-inflammatory effect. Salicin is the active constituent from which aspirin was first synthesized. White willow bark is used for rheumatic complaints, arthritis, headaches, diarrhoea and dysentery. Willow bark also treats fevers, edema and aftereffects of worms.

To make tea, steep 3 teaspoons of the bark in one cup of cold water for 2-5 hours, boil for 1 min and strain.

Willow also is available as a powder. The dose is 1 teaspoon, x3 times a day in tea or capsules. The tincture can be taken in 10-20 drop doses x4 times a day.

Cautions: Willow bark is not a substitute for aspirin. If you are taking aspirin as an anti-coagulant, to keep the blood thin, it is important to continue as willow does not have this property.

Ogam Channel Healing Guide

Spiritual/Mind: Abusive situations Bitterness Confidence Clairvoyance Dreaming Visions Divination Female Sexuality Find buried emotions Grief Hysteria Inspiration Jealousy Lunar cycles Magic Negative thoughts Negative vibrations Neglect Nervous-ness Positive hidden influences Resentfulness Sadness

Head: Fevers Headaches Hysteria Neuralgia Pain relief

Chest: Blood thinning Colds Influenza Pneumonia Respiratory infections Whooping cough

Stomach: Gastrointestinal-distress Diarrhoea Dysentery Worms

Urinary: Bladder complaints Urinary tract complaints

Women's Cycle: Menstrual pain, cramps, mood swings Fertility Internal hormone -balance

Skin: Skin complaints   External wounds

Muscles: Aching muscles   Lower back ache

Joints: Rheumatism

General: Gout

Flower Remedy

Willow Flower Essence is used as a remedy for people who feel resentful and bitter; people who begrudge others (or circumstances) for their problems and are prone to resentment and self-pity. Its essence apparently alleviates bitterness. Willow leaves act as charms against jealousy. The remedy encourages the rebirth of optimism and faith with an understanding that negative thought may attract the issues we complain about.

Notes

Willow is linked with divining rods used in dowsing for water. It is usually found next to flowing water and so has an innate association with it. There is an obvious connection to clairvoyance, seership, divination and psychic powers.

Folklore

Willow is one of four tree species used ritually during the Jewish holiday of *Sukkot*. In Buddhism, a willow branch is one of the chief attributes of *Kwan Yin*, the *bodhisattva* of compassion. Christian churches in northwestern Europe and Ukraine and Bulgaria often used willow branches in the ceremonies on Palm Sunday in place of palms.

The witches' broom is traditionally made from three trees. The stave from ash, for protection; birch twigs for the broom itself to expel evil spirits and the besom is bound with willow to honour Hecate.

Willow has been used in the Sacred Pipes and the tobacco blends of many Native Americans because it is thought to be very effective in carrying messages to the Great Spirit. Willow has been planted by Sacred Wells to help pull Earth energies into the water and hold them there for those who wish to take magical draughts.

The weeping willow is a common sign of mourning. In the UK, no builders in the Fens used sawn willow for building, as it was traditionally the wood of the gallows and using it was said to bring disaster to the family. One explanation for why the willow weeps is because it hung over the heads of the apostles while they waited and slept when our Lord suffered his agony, and ever after it has wept.

In mythology, willow was sacred to Hera, Hecate, Circe and Persephone; all of goddesses of the underworld. Orpheus received his gifts of eloquence and communication because he carried willow branches with him through the Underworld.

In Celtic mythology, willow represents death goddesses. It is therefore good for magical work involving the dark self or hidden parts of the psyche. People used spikes of willow among their vegetables to protect crops and animals.

Some people believed that striking children or animals with a willow stick stunted their growth. Ancient Chinese hung willow branches above the door to keep evil spirits away. In Essex they would do the same thing to keep witches at bay.

The phrase *to knock on wood* refers to the wood of a willow tree. If you have a secret, tell a willow, and it'll trap it in its wood. *Wind in the willows* refers to the elves whispering among themselves in willows as people walked underneath. It is bad luck to burn willow wood. Weeping willows with branches growing up instead of down were even more unlucky, and so people were advised to cut them down. In Ireland they used willows to make harps and claimed that the willow's souls spoke through music. In Bohemia, it was believed that the willow's soul would die if the tree was cut down.

A Greek proverb suggests men should, when passing a water willow, pause to touch and smell it, otherwise they will lose their sweetheart. A Japanese superstition advises anyone with a toothache to stick needles into a willow tree as then the spirit of the tree will cure the toothache.

Ash   Nuin   Transformation

Nuin (Nion) corresponds to the letter N in the Ogam alphabet and is associated with the Ash tree. The symbol represents the connection between the inner self to the outer worlds. A symbol of creativity and all that transitions between these points.

Nuin pronounced: Nee-uhn

Status: Peasant-tree

Element: Fire

Gender: Masculine

Celtic Fifth Month: March

Powers: Nuin links the above with the below and the inner with the outer.

Keywords

Links, understanding, control, focus, awareness, action, transform, destiny, magic potency, healing and health, protection, love, women's mysteries, prophetic dreams and prosperity.

Deities associated with Ash

Odin, Woden, Thor, Poseidon, Nemesis, Achilles, Andrasteia, Neptune, Gwydion, Mars. Frigg, Eostre, Hel/Holle, Minerva.

Tree description

Ash trees are medium to large trees and widespread in Europe. Some are evergreen, but most are deciduous. The ash tree tends to form an untidy crown which include many dead branches. It can grow between 20-40m high with its trunk tending to be long and straight.

The bark when young is smooth and grey, but as it ages it splits into long ridges and fissures. The twigs give a grey shine in winter and bear very distinctive buds, which are sooty or velvety in appearance and can look like the shape of a Bishop's Mitre. It has light-green, oval shaped, pinnate leaves with 9 – 13 leaflets in pairs, with one at the tip. The leaflets are pointed and toothed, with hairs on the lower surface. It comes to leaf late in spring, and are shed in autumn, usually still green.

The flowers of the ash may be male, female or hermaphrodite, as indeed may be the whole tree. Flowers appear in April before the leaves and if male, are dark purple in colour. The fruit is known as a samara, or *keys*, in English. They are shed in October and are set in a long narrow brown wing.

Uses

Ash is a hardwood and is hard, dense, and very strong but has an elasticity to it, making it just right for making bows, tool handles, baseball bats and anything else that demands high strength and resilience. Because it is robust, looks good, and has great flexibility, Ash is widely used for staircases. They are extremely hard-wearing, can be worked on to produce curved stair parts such as curled handrails and intricately shaped balusters.

Ash is used as material for electric guitar bodies. It has become known for its bright, cutting tone and sustaining quality. Some Fender Stratocasters and Telecasters are made of ash, as an alternative to alder. They are also used for making drum shells.

It is known for its great finishing qualities, extremely good machining qualities, and is easy to use with nails, screws, and glue. It is used in interior joinery, including ash veneers and used extensively in office furniture. The Morgan Motor Company manufacture sports cars with frames made of ash. It was also used for early aircraft construction. It is a light wood and burns easily, so is used for starting fires and barbecues. The leaves of ash are fed to cattle, goats, and rabbits. If cut in the autumn, its branches can be a valuable winter supply for domestic animals.

Interesting Spiritual Info

The Ash is the World tree. It connects the past, present and future and is the link between the microcosm and macrocosm. As above so below, the cosmos is reflected in both mankind and earthly things. The inner workings within your different levels have a reaction in the outer. A sacred Druid tree, one of three; oak, ash and thorn. It is said that Druids used wands of ash because of its straight grain.

Ash can be used for healing, general and solar magic, also in spells requiring strength of purpose and focus, it specifies the links between the inner and outer worlds. Put ash leaves under your pillow to help stimulate psychic dreams.

Tree Medicines

The bark of the ash tree trunk and the bark of its roots both have astringent properties and have been used in decoctions to aid fevers, remove obstructions in the liver and spleen. It is also good for rheumatism and arthritis. The leaves which are diuretic and diaphoretic and promote sweating are used for their purgative qualities and also as a cure for jaundice.

The ash's tree bark, roots and leaves have also traditionally been used to treat external cancerous growths, used as pain killers, as an anti-inflammatory for gout, rheumatism, arthritis and for intestinal worms.

Modern medical research has also shown that seed extract may in the future be used for diabetes and as a means to regulate uric acid in the blood in the treatment of gout. Fraxtin, a bioflavonoid in the tree has strong antioxidant properties, and a secoiridoid glycoside in the tree, excelsioside, has exhibited free radical scavenging activities, so will combat the growth of cancer cells.

It also contains quercetin, another bioflavonoid with antioxidant properties, and oleuropein which is also present in olive oil, this has anti-inflammatory properties, is cardio-protective and also has anti-cancer, antimicrobial anti-artherogenic, and antiviral qualities. It can also be used as a compress on suppurating cuts and sores

Herbal Medicine: Fraxinus excelsior

Common Name: Ash.

Parts Used: Bark and leaves.

Overview: It can be used as a substitute for quinine in intermittent fevers. It is said to help clear obstructions from the spleen and liver.

Simmer 2 tablespoons of bark for 20 mins in one cup of water and take a quarter of a cup 4 times a day.

The leaves act as a laxative. Steep 2 tablespoons of the leaf in one cup of water for 20 mins, take one quarter of a cup per day.

It has recently become a constituent of an effective anti-inflammatory medicine (this includes ash bark mixed with the tree *Populus tremula* and the herb *Solidago virgaurea*).

Cautions: None found.

Ogam Channel Healing Guide

Spiritual/Mind: Ability to focus   Action   Awareness   Clarity of mind   Control Destiny   Fear based worries   Harmony to self-Healing   Identity worries   Inner/ outer issues/ problems etc   Love   Magic potency   Transformation   Prophetic –dreams   Prosperity   Protection   Understanding

Head: Fevers

Chest: Heart Love Worries

Organs: Liver complaints   Spleen

Women's Cycles: Women's mysteries

Skin: Cuts/ sores

Joints: Arthritis   Rheumatism

Cancer: Cancer (general) External cancer growths

General: Gout

Flower Remedies

The Ash Tree essence helps bring illumination and clear clarity to the mind. It encourages thoughtful consideration in times of severe inner conflict, helps to calm hostile thoughts, and iron out any confusion about one's sense of identity. It brings a greater harmony to the self and nature.

Notes

The ash was noted as a powerful Druid wand which was well known for its magic abilities like bringing storms to bear, directing curses at their enemies, becoming invisible, turning people into animals (good and bad), healing and calling up their allies.

Folklore

In Greek mythology, the Meliae were nymphs of the ash, just as dryads were nymphs of the oak tree. The ancient Greek goddess Nemesis carried an ash branch as a symbol of the divine instrument of the justice of the gods. She measured out mortal happiness or misery, ensuring that fortune was shared out equally amongst all people and not kept by the few.

The ash exudes a sugary substance that is suggested to have been fermented to create the Norse Mead of Inspiration. Yggdrasil is an immense mythical tree that plays a central role in Norse cosmology. Yggdrasill is the tree of life, and is an eternal green ash tree, whose branches connect all of the nine worlds and extends up to and above the heavens. Yggdrasil has three large roots. The first root is in Asgard, the home of the Gods and it is just next to the well-named Urd, where the gods and goddesses have their daily meetings. The second root from Yggdrasil goes all the way down to Jotunheim, the land of the giants, next to Mimir's well. The third root travels down to Nifleim, close to the well, Hvergelmir. It is here that Nidhug, a dragon, chews on it. Nidhug also sucks blood from the dead bodies which come to Hel. At the very top of Yggdrasil lives an eagle, who is an enemy of Nidhug and truly despise one another. There is a squirrel called Ratatosk, who runs up and down the tree all day long revealing what the other has said about itself, so fuelling the hatred between dragon and eagle. Odin hung himself upon Yggdrasil and uses it to ride (journey) through the nine worlds.

There are European folklore stories about snakes repelled by ash leaves, or a circle drawn by an ash branch. In Irish folklore, it is claimed that shadows from an ash tree would damage crops. In Cheshire, ash was said to be used to cure warts and rickets. In Sussex, the ash tree and the elm tree were known as *widow makers* because large branches would often drop without warning. My good friend, Mike Downs, who is a tree surgeon, told me that all trees are potential widow makers, as most will have dead wood attached until released due to heavy winds (note to all: please don't shelter under any large tree in a high wind)!

11

Hawthorn   Huathe   (Obstacles)

Huathe corresponds to the letter H in the Ogam alphabet and is associated with the Hawthorn tree. The symbol represents the cleansing, protection and fertility.

Huathe pronounced: hOO-uh

Status: Peasant-tree

Element: Fire

Gender: Masculine

Celtic Sixth Month: April

Powers: Huathe creates a sacred space for protection, cleansing and creation.

Keywords

Cleansing and chastity, protection, obstacles, obstructions, purity, compensation, female sexuality, fertility, the power of magical sexuality, inner journeys, intuition and happiness.

Deities associated with Hawthorn

Flora, Olwen, Blodeuwedd, Hera, Cardea and Hymen (god of marriage), Maia, Belenus.

Tree Description

The Hawthorn tree is native to Northern Europe, Asia and North America. Hawthorn is usually seen as a dense thorny shrub, or a small tree, mostly growing to 5–15 m tall, with small pome fruit and thorny branches. It is common to all soils except the most acidic and is found in hedgerows mainly in the countryside.

Its bark is usually bright brown and flaking, although it develops shallow fissures with narrow ridges in older trees. The leaves vary their shape across the species but are usually lobed or have serrated margins and have 3-4 pairs of lobes. The flowers appear in dense clusters around May-June. They are about 10-15mm across, white, but tend to turn pink as they mature. You may find some with pink or double-flowered forms. Each flower will only have one style and one ovary. The fruit, known as a haw, is deep red, sometimes purple, and berry-like. They will grow for as long as they can. The thorns which are small sharp-tipped branches are usually 1–3 cm long.

Uses

Birds and mammals eat the haws during the winter months. The plant also provides shelter, and the flowers are a food source for the many nectar-feeding insects. The haws or fruits of the common hawthorn are edible, but the flavour has been compared to over-ripe apples. In the UK, they are sometimes made into jelly or homemade wines. In rural England, the young leaves and flower buds are known as *bread and cheese*, as they are edible and if picked in spring can be used in salads. Hawthorn hedges are very prevalent in the countryside, being used as borders for fields and roadways.

Interesting Spiritual Information

The Hawthorn is also known as the May Tree and White Thorn. Wands made from hawthorn are of great power. It represents cleansing and chastity; it brings protection from the inner magical realms. It also is about sitting in a state of restraint and keeping yourself to yourself.

A time for reflection before setting out on physical activity. Spiritual fertilization is needed within this time.

The Fey (Earth Spirits/Fairy Folk) are especially drawn to hawthorn as they see it as sacred. Hawthorn wood creates the hottest fires and wands used in magic work hold the greatest power. The Greeks and Romans saw the Hawthorn as symbolic of both hope and marriage, whilst in medieval Europe it was associated with witchcraft and considered unlucky.

Tree Medicine

Hawthorn is used for diseases of the heart and blood vessels such as congestive heart failure (CHF), chest pain, and irregular heartbeat. It is also used to treat both low blood pressure and high blood pressure, "hardening of the arteries" (atherosclerosis), and high cholesterol. So far, research suggests that hawthorn might be effective in treating congestive heart failure, but there hasn't been enough research on other heart-related uses to know if it is effective for them.

Some people use hawthorn for digestive system complaints such as indigestion, diarrhoea, and stomach pain. It is also used to reduce anxiety, as a sedative, to increase urine output, and for menstrual problems. Hawthorn is also used to treat tapeworm and other intestinal infections.

Some people apply hawthorn to the skin for boils, sores, and ulcers. Hawthorn preparations are used as a wash for sores, itching, and frostbite.

You will find hawthorn among the ingredients in candied fruit slices, jam, jelly, and wine.

Before taking hawthorn, talk with your healthcare professional if you take any medications. It has major interactions with several prescription medications.

How does it work?

Hawthorn can help improve the amount of blood pumped out of the heart during contractions, widen the blood vessels, and increase the transmission of nerve signals.

Hawthorn also seems to have blood pressure-lowering activity, according to early research. It seems to cause relaxing of the blood vessels farther from the heart. It seems that this effect is due to a component in hawthorn called proanthocyanidin.

Research suggests that hawthorn can lower cholesterol, low density lipoprotein (LDL, or "bad cholesterol"), and triglycerides (fats in the blood). It seems to lower accumulation of fats in the liver and the aorta (the largest artery in the body, located near the heart). Hawthorn fruit extract may lower cholesterol by increasing the excretion of bile, reducing the formation of cholesterol, and enhancing the receptors for LDLs. It also seems to have antioxidant activity.

Used as a sedative – as it can regulate blood pressure, it also eases diarrhoea, dysentery, kidney inflammations and disorders. Tea from its leaves and blossoms aid with anxiety, appetite loss and poor circulation. An extract of hawthorn is used in treating chronic heart failure or as a useful remedy in the treatment of cardiovascular disease. Cardiac tonic, hypotensive/blood pressure normalizing, antioxidant.

Phytochemicals found in hawthorn include tannins, flavonids, oligomeric proanthocyanidins, and phenolic acids to help protect myocardium against oxidative damage, it prevents oxidized cholesterol from accumulating in vessel walls.

Its dried fruits are used in traditional Chinese medicine, primarily as a digestive aid.

A Japanese hawthorn is used in a similar manner. Other species are used in herbal medicine where the plant is believed to strengthen cardiovascular function. Hawthorns help digestion, strengthen the intestines and fight low blood pressure.

Herbal Medicine: Crataegus species

Common Names: Hawthorn (May tree)

Parts Used: Flowers, fruits, leaves.

Overview: Hawthorn achieves great healing effects in a gentle, supportive way. Tea made from the leaves and flowers is pleasant and can be taken daily to help treat a variety of heart and circulatory problems. They contain potent chemical compounds that act as antioxidants to protect the heart's tissues from damage. The berry is useful for almost any heart condition including cholesterol issues and lowering blood pressure. The berry is also good for nerves and insomnia. Berries are simmered or tinctured.

Simmer 2 teaspoons of berries per cup of water for 20 mins and the dose is a quarter of a cup x4 a day.

Tinctured berries take 10-20 drops x4 times a day. Tincture, 1.5 in 45% alcohol. Take 1-2ml x3 times daily.

The flowers are taken as tea to benefit the heart. Steep 2 tablespoons of flowers per cup of water for 20 mins, and the dose is a quarter of a cup x4 times a day.

Cautions: Hawthorn is generally considered safe but has an effect on the angiotensin-converting enzyme, involved in the regulation of blood pressure, so should not be taken alongside conventional drugs. People with low blood pressure should avoid Hawthorn as it may lower the pressure still further. Do not use hawthorn if pregnant.

Ogam Channel Healing Guide

Spiritual/Mind: Being (Mindfulness) Clarity Cleansing Chastity Clearing obstacles or obstructions in your way Courage Fertility Happiness Inner journeys Insomnia Intuition Nerves Protection Purity Self-love Female sexuality Female: the power of magical sexuality Peacefulness

Head/Neck: Appetite loss Nausea Stress relief used as a sedative Restlessness, anxiety, AD(H)D

Heart: Anxiety Congestive Heart Failure Heart Failure Coronary artery disease Elevated blood lipids (cholesterol, triglyerides) Poor circulation Post-Heart Attacks Regulates blood pressure

Stomach: Digestion Eases diarrhoea/ dysentery Intestines

Kidney: Kidney inflammations and disorders

Flower Remedies

Hawthorne flower essence helps open the heart to be able to give and to receive love, also extremely helpful in healing heartache. It encourages self-love and self-acceptance and helps us to develop courage.

Notes

The hawthorn is one of the three sacred fairy trees of Britain: oak, ash and thorn. Where all three grow it is said one may see fairies. It marks a magical barrier. It brings a testing to those who wish to pass it, as in the prince looking to find his princess, a pilgrim on his life journey, a person wishing to access his money from the bank, someone enjoying his mental state. The desire to move forward is being thwarted with this obstacle. It gives you a dilemma of trying to press through and only getting hurt or to rethink and find a new route round.

Folklore

The hawthorn was allegedly carried by ancient Greeks in wedding processions (as an emblem of hope) and used to decorate the altar of Hymenaios.

There was an old superstition in Great Britain and Ireland, that bad luck would follow you, if you uprooted a hawthorn. This was because it was thought that the crown of thorns worn by Jesus came from a hawthorn tree. In medieval times it was thought that the Glastonbury thorn, which flowers twice annually, was supposed to have come from the walking stick planted by Joseph of Arimathea. During the English Reformation, it was said that the original tree was destroyed, but some cultivars survived.

In Celtic Lore, the hawthorn trunk was used for carving inscriptions. It has been said that it can heal a broken heart. According to Gaelic folklore, the hawthorn marks the entrance to the otherworld and is strongly associated with the fairies. Thomas the Rhymer met the Faerie Queen under a hawthorn tree and ended up staying with her in the Underworld for seven years. They are also found close to holy wells and pilgrims would often tie strips of cloth to their branches as part of their healing ritual (this is still done today at sacred sites). In Ireland there was a common expression concerning the hawthorn, 'When all fruit fails, welcome haws.'

In the Victorian era, the hawthorn represented hope as in the language of flowers. In Serbian and Croatian folklore, should you need to slay a vampire, you should use stakes made from hawthorn.

Oak   Diur   (Duration)

Duir corresponds to the letter D in the Ogam alphabet and is associated with the Oak tree. The symbol represents the strength, the doorway to wisdom and self-confidence.

Duir pronounced: dehr

Status: Chieftain-tree

Element: Fire

Gender: Masculine

Celtic Seventh Month: May

Powers: Diur is the doorway to the mysteries, guardian of histories and solid protection.

Keywords

Solid protection, doorway, magical strength, security, truth, insight, inner knowledge, ability to bar or open, endurance, maturity, nobility and goodwill.

Deities associated with Oak

Dione, Diana, Rhea, Cybele, Circe, Athene, Demeter, Brigid, Bridhe, St Brigit, Blodeuwedd and Cerridwen. Zeus, Jupiter, Hercules, Pan, Jehovah, Esus, Odin, Thor, Dagda and Herne.

Tree Description

Oak trees are native to the Northern Hemisphere and include deciduous and evergreen species. English oak can vary in size and shape, in extreme cases can reach 45m high, but usually less than 20m high when mature. Its bark is finely cracked and has ridges. Oaks have short stalked spirally arranged leaves, with lobate margins in many species; some have serrated leaves or entire leaves with smooth margins. Many deciduous species do not drop their dead leaves until spring. In spring, a single oak tree produces both male flowers in the form of catkins and small female flowers. The fruit is an acorn or oak nut borne in a cup-like structure known as a cupule; each acorn contains one seed (rarely two or three) and takes 6–18 months to mature, depending on their species. The acorns and leaves contain tannic acid, which helps to guard from fungi and insects.

Uses

Oak wood is one of the strongest of woods. It is very resistant to insect and fungal attack due to its high tannin content. It used as floorboards, staircases and oak planking was common on high status Viking long ships in the 9th and 10th centuries. Wide boards of oak have been used in interior paneling of prestigious buildings such as the debating chamber of the House of Commons in London. It is also used in the construction of fine furniture, flooring and veneer production.

Oak wood was used in Europe for the construction of navel and regular merchant ships up until the 19th century, and in the construction of European timber-framed buildings. Oak barrels help in the aging of whisky, brandy, sherry and wines. Oak barrels, charred before use, contribute to the colour, taste, and aroma of the contents, giving a desirable oaky vanilla flavour to these drinks. Oak wood chips are used for smoking fish, meat, cheeses, and other foods.

Japanese oak is used by Yamaha in the making of professional drums. Compared to the traditional drum materials of maple and birch, the higher density of oak gives them a brighter and louder tone. In India, besides using oak for firewood and timber, certain country people use it to make agricultural implements. The leaves are often used as fodder during lean periods and as bedding for livestock. Acorns were also used as pig food. The bark of the cork oak is used to produce wine stoppers (corks). The bark of the white oak is dried and used in medical preparations.

Oak bark, which is rich in tannin, is used by tanners for tanning leather. Acorns are used for making flour or roasted for acorn coffee. Oak galls were used as a main ingredient in iron gall ink, a kind of manuscript ink and harvested at a specific time in the year. In Korea, oak bark is used to make shingles for traditional roofing construction.

Interesting Spiritual Information

One of the three sacred Druidic trees, oak, ash and thorn. Oak is king in the forest, it is solid, and a survivor of many lightning strikes. It acts as a marker point, boundary and refuge. A doorway into which the pilgrim can cross to explore his spirituality in depth and with help.

It is associated with protection spells, strength, success, stability, healing, fertility, health, money, potency and good luck. It has been considered sacred by most cultures that have encountered it, but the Celts especially adored it, from its size, long life, and wholesome acorns.

The oak is also often associated with gods of thunder and lightning, such as Thor and Zeus. During storms, the oak is quite often hit by lightning but lives on to fight another day. For fertility themes, acorns that were gathered at night were seen to hold the greatest fertility powers. Druids were known to teach under its illustrious branches and were said to listen to its rustling oak leaves for divinatory messages. The energy of the oak is strong and fills you with positivity. A good tree to be with when you need to make a decision.

Tree Medicine

It is mainly the bark which is used in medicine. Its action is slightly tonic, strongly astringent, due to high tannin content and used as an antiseptic. Like other astringents, it has been recommended in agues and haemorrhages, and is a good substitute for quinine in intermittent fever.

It is useful for stopping chronic diarrhoea and dysentery, either alone or in conjunction with aromatics. A decoction made from bark can be used externally as a gargle in chronic sore throat with relaxed uvula, and also as a fomentation. It is also serviceable as an injection for leucorrhoea and applied locally to bleeding gums and piles.

Oak bark when finely powdered and inhaled freely, has proved very beneficial in early stages of consumption. A remedial snuff is also made from the freshly collected oak bark, dried and reduced to a fine powder.

The thin skin covering the acorn has proved effectual in staying spitting of blood, and the powder of the acorn taken in wine is considered a good diuretic. A decoction of acorns and oak bark, made with milk, was considered an antidote to poisonous herbs and medicines.

The distilled water of the oak bud was also thought to work well inwardly or outwardly to ease inflammation. Bruised leaves have been applied to help heal wounds and burning oak leaves have been used to purify the atmosphere.

Herbal Medicine: Quercus robur

Common Names: Oak, common oak, English oak, French oak.

Parts used: Bark, buds, leaves.

Overview: Its healing effects are due to the tannins that the bark contains which are useful in the treatment of diarrhoea and rectal issues, as well as menstrual irregularities and bloody urine.

A tea of oak buds is very good for the liver, steep two teaspoons per cup of water for 20 mins.

To help shrink varicose veins, drink as a tea and apple externally in fomentation.

Tea will bring down fevers, treat diarrhoea and will make a wash for sores. Use just three cups a day.

Use as a gargle for treating mouth sores, mouth inflammations and sore throats.

As an astringent it will stop internal bleeding.

For vaginal infections gather oak leaves (before Midsummer) and steep one tablespoon per quart of water for 30 mins and use as a douche.

Simmer the bark in salves for haemorrhoids.

Powdered bark can be taken as snuff for nasal polyps.

Cautions: Oak bark is highly astringent and can actively decrease the amount of nutrients absorbed from your diet. When taken internally (for diarrhoea) it should only be used for 3-4 days at the most.

Ogam Channel Healing Guide

Spiritual/Mind: Ability to bar or open   Building up your will   Courage and endurance   Doorway to spirituality   Endurance   Inner knowledge   Insight   Magical strength   Maturity   Nobility/goodwill   Ideal for making wise decisions   Purifying the body   Security   Self-determination   Solid Protection   Strength in heart   Truth

Head/Neck: Mouth   Mouth sores   Nasal polyps   Nose bleeds   Spitting blood

Throat: Sore throats

Chest: Pepping up your energy   Consumption

Stomach: Diarrhoea   Stomach complaints

Liver: Liver problems

Female Cycle: Menstrual issues   Vaginal complaints

Skin: Sores   Wounds

Bowels: Haemorrhoids   Rectal issues

General: Agues   Internal bleeding   Haemorrhaging

Flower Remedies

Oak is the remedy for strong people who stand up against too much adversity in their life. Whilst they own the ability to keep going on in a determined way, they do so without pause or thought of rest. There might be a number of people relying on them and so they own a strong moral and sense of duty. They can easily feel frustrated and unhappy if an illness suddenly comes and stops them doing as they would like. In this aspect they can be extremely stubborn. The oak remedy helps them stay strong when up against it as well as realising there are definitely times when it is wise to let go and heal themselves rather than crack and break.

Notes

The oak tree is the king of the woodlands it lives in. It is well known for its endurance, strength and nobility. It lives for several hundred years and can attract lightning in storms but tends to survive strikes. This ability has linked it with many thunder gods across pagan Europe.

Folklore

The oak tree has been respected by many of the major cultures of Europe for the last few thousand years. The Greeks, Romans, Celts and Teutonic tribes all associated their main Gods (Zeus, Jupiter, Dagda, and Thor), with the sacred oak. It is no coincidence that all of these gods also had dominion over rain, thunder and lightning, as above all other trees, the oak is most likely to be hit by lightning.

The Druids where renowned for worshipping and teaching in oak groves (the word, Druid, was probably a Gaelic derivation of their word for oak, Duir, and meant men of the oaks). Mistletoe, probably the Druid's most potent and magical healing plant, frequently grew on oak trees. The fact it grew on this sacred tree indicated to them that it was a special plant, placed there by the hand of God.

Oak leaves have for many centuries been used by the military as decorative icons of military prowess around the world. Ancient kings wore crowns of oak leaves, symbols of the god they represented as kings on Earth. Roman commanders were also donned with crowns of oak leaves during victory parades.

The Tudors used oak because of its strength and durability not only in timbered houses, but also for the Royal Navy and their mighty ships for many years.

Artists frequently choose it as a source of their work due to its even-grained, honey-coloured beauty in carving and turning. The bark of the oak was highly valued by the leather tanning industry because of its high tannin content. During the Industrial Revolution, large volumes were sent from specially managed oak woodlands in the north west of Scotland to Glasgow for this purpose.

The bark yields a brown dye, and oak galls gave the strong black dye from which ink was made. A tonic derived from boiling the bark was used to treat harness sores on horses.

Because of the oak's size, and the fact it makes grand presence in a community, much of its folklore concerns specific, individual oak trees. Many parishes used to contain a *Gospel Oak*, where part of the Gospel was read out during the Beating of the Bounds ceremonies at Rogantide in spring.

There are two ancient oaks in Somerset, named after the last male and female giants to roam Britain. They are called Gog and Magog and are said by some to be the remnants of an oak-lined processional route up to the nearby Glastonbury Tor.

The Major Oak in Sherwood Forest is supposed to be the Robin Hood tree from folklore and has become a popular tourist attraction.

At Midsummer, the oak hands its power over to the holly tree and it is said it is a battle between rival gods for the hand of the earth-goddess (See notes for the holly tree).

Holly   Tinne   (Challenge)

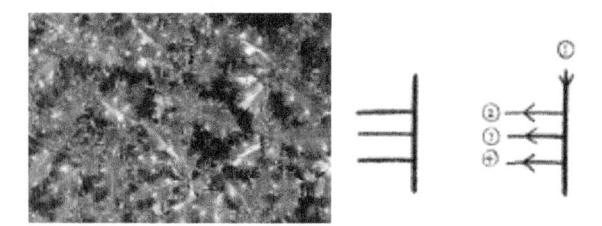

Tinne corresponds to the letter T in the Ogam alphabet and is associated with the Holly tree. This symbol represents courage, balance and power.

Tinne pronounced: TINg-yuh

Status: Shrub

Element: Fire

Gender: Masculine

Celtic Eighth Month: June

Powers: Holly is tough and best used in a fight.

Keywords

The Holly King, best in the fight, energy, guidance for future problems, balance, strong in arguments, justice, challenge, directness, boldness, power, emotional + spiritual tests.

Deities associated with Holly

Tannus, Taranis, Thor (the thunder gods), Freya, Lugh.

Tree Description

The Holly species are evergreen or deciduous trees, shrubs, and climbers from tropics to temperate zones worldwide. Holly is a very distinct tree and can grow as high as 20m but is typically used as a hedgerow tree. It can also be used for ornamental and shelter reasons. The bark of the tree is smooth and grey. The leaves are tough, dark green and glossy, frequently lobed with a spiny leaf margin. The upper leaves and sometimes, although rarely, all or most of the tree's leaves may be spineless and almost smooth edged.

The flowers are small, 7-8mm across, greenish white, with four petals and fragrant. Generally, the male and female flowers are found on different plants, around May time. They range in colour from red to brown to black. The berries contain around four seeds each, ripen in winter and can cause vomiting and diarrhea when ingested by humans, but are an important food source for birds which help with the dispersal of its seeds.

Uses

Certain cultures use certain holly leaves to make tea. Many of the holly species are widely used as ornamental plants in gardens and parks. Hollies are often used for hedges; the spiny leaves make them difficult to penetrate, and they take well to pruning and shaping. In many western Christian cultures, holly is seen and used a traditional Christmas decoration, used in wreaths and pictured on Christmas cards.

In heraldry, holly is used to symbolize truth. The Norwegian municipality of Stord has a yellow twig of holly in its Coat-of-arms. Holly wood is the whitest of all woods, it is heavy, hard and fine grained. Artists and carpenters use it for engraving, carving or to make furniture. It can be stained and polished to make walking sticks.

Coppicing allowed the hard, white, close-grained wood to be used for inlaid marquetry, chess pieces and tool handles. Holly wood makes good firewood and burns with a strong heat and was used by smiths and weapon makers. It was often used as wooden spear shafts which gave good balance and excellent sense of direction. The coppicing of holly trees also allowed its leaves to be used as winter feed for livestock. Some farmers would ground the pricklier leaves to make them more palatable.

Interesting Spiritual Information

Holly is associated with the death and rebirth symbolism of winter in both Pagan and Christian lore. It is important to the Winter Solstice. The Holly is male and symbolizes paternity and fatherhood. It is a potent life symbol and gives you balance and a directness for your focus. It also is associated with protection magic, prophesy, healing, animals, sex, invulnerability, watchfulness, good luck, holiness and consecration. It was one of three woods used to make chariot wheels as well as in the shaft of a spear. The holly's qualities of directed balance and vigour, to fight if the cause be just can be seen in these uses. Holly can be used to aid in the passage of death.

Tree Medicine

Holly leaves are used to aid several health disorders. They are used as a remedy to hypertension, also referred to as high blood pressure. The leaves can have a calming effect and have been known to ease blood circulation. They have also been used to treat fever, rheumatism and digestive issues. Some species are utilized for their emetic properties, and others used to assist with symptoms such as joint pain and swelling. Leaves when dried can be used as tea for fevers, bronchitis, bladder problems and gout. Tea made from leaves are used to alleviate measles, colds, flu, and pneumonia. The leaves are also used to stimulate the heart, empty and cleanse the bowels, and increase urine flow.

They can be used externally for sores and itching. Holly leaf extract is sometimes used to combat jaundice, dizziness and emotional problems. In some cases, holly is even utilized as a method of fighting heart disease. The plant has been employed for centuries as an herbal remedy. Tea made from the holly bark was once used for treating malaria and epilepsy. Its berries have strong laxative, emetic, and diuretic qualities when ingested.

Herbal Medicine: Ilex aquifolium

Common Names: Holly, Holy tree.

Parts used: Bark, berries, leaves, roots.

Overview: In the past the leaves were used as a remedy for infectious diseases including malaria and smallpox. In North America the Micmac tribe used the roots for coughs and tuberculosis. Nowadays the leaf is dried and used as a tea for fevers, bronchitis, bladder problems and gout.

Steep half an ounce of chopped up leaf and boil in water for 20 mins. Take up to one cup a day.

The juice of the fresh leaf can be helpful in jaundice, take 1 spoonful per day.

Cautions: The berries can cause vomiting, diarrhoea, drowsiness and are poisonous.

Ogam Channel Healing Guide

Spiritual/Mind: Absence of love   Balance of focus   Boldness   Challenges   Courage   Directing-focus   Emotional-problems   Emotional-tests   Fatherhood   Generosity of spirit   Good luck   Guidance for future problems   Jealousy   Male sexuality   Negative energy   Protection   Hatred towards others   Justice   Male-energy   Negative thoughts/energy   Spiritual tests   Spite towards others   Strong in arguments

Head/Neck: Dizziness   Epilepsy

Chest: Aid in high blood pressure   Bronchitis and tuberculosis   Colds/ flu   External sores and itching   Fevers   Heart   Malaria   Measles   Pneumonia

Stomach: Emetic and diuretic qualities   Digestion   Laxative

Urinary: Bladder complaints

Skin: Sores (itching)

Joints: Joint pain (swelling)Rheumatism

Bowels: Bowl cleansing

General: Gout   Jaundice   Smallpox

Flower Remedy

Holly is the ideal remedy for when you are directing very negative, aggressive feelings such as hatred, suspicion, envy and spite towards others. The problem is simply an absence of love, and the remedy works to encourage our generosity of spirit and an openness towards others.

Notes

In Celtic mythology, the Holly King ruled over half the year from summer to the winter solstice, then the Oak King would defeat the Holly King and rule through until the summer solstice again. There are many poems and songs dedicated to this event. The Holly and Oak Kings were seen as two aspects of the Nature God and were sometimes integrated into plays performed by the Mummers' around Yuletide. The Holly King was depicted as a giant man covered in holly leaves and branches, his club was made from a whole holly bush and he has been seen by some to be the precursor of the Green Man.

Folklore

The holly was seen to have protective properties, which explained why across the land there many taboos were against cutting down a whole tree. They were also left uncut in hedges when trimmed. This was to stop witches who were well known to run along the tops of them.

However, it is better known as a way of helping farmers establish lines of sight during winter ploughing by checking in on their distinctive evergreen shapes.

Taken into your home in winter, it can shelter the Fey without harm to mortals. The only warning is that it should be carefully removed by Imbolc eve, 31st January, as if there is anything left, it can bring misfortune. However, due to its light-reflecting leaves and colourful berries it can lift people's spirits. Depending on whether smooth or prickly leaved holly was brought into the home, would dictate whether the husband or wife ruled the household for the coming year.

As we know, the holly king takes over from the oak king at Midsummer and represents the tenacity of life, it is the green of nature carried through the seasons, guarded by his spiky holly club. The Druids were aware of this property and apparently wore holly in their hair because its leaves offered protection against evil spirits.

Christians have used heavy symbolism within its form; The sharp leaves represent the crown of thorns worn by Jesus; the red berries are the drops of blood shed for salvation; and the *flame* shape of the leaves, reveal God's burning love for His people. There was a time when holly was referred to as *Christmas* and in pre-Victorian times, they used holly bushes as Christmas trees. In the well-known Christmas carol, The Holly and the Ivy, the holly represents Jesus, and the ivy represents the Virgin Mary.

Folklore suggested that this wood had an affinity for *control*, which explained why the whips for ploughmen and coaches were made from coppiced holly. Holly trees were traditionally planted near houses as it was known to be good protection from lightning strikes. In European mythology, holly was also associated with thunder gods such as Thor and Taranis. It has been scientifically proven that the spines on holly leaves can act as miniature lightning conductors, so protecting the tree and other nearby objects.

Hazel   Coll   (Enlightenment)

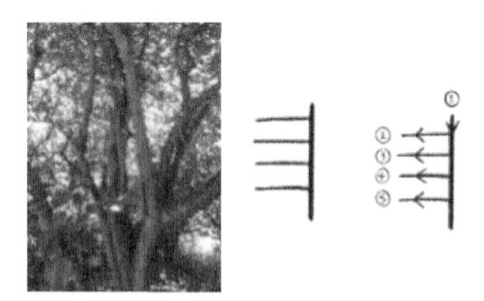

Coll corresponds to the letter C in the Ogam alphabet and is associated with the Hazel tree. This symbol represents wisdom, creativity and enlightenment.

Coll pronounced: kuhl

Status: Chieftain-tree

Element: Air

Gender: Masculine

Celtic Ninth Month: July

Powers: Coll used in the search for illumination in both creative and divine messages.

Keywords

Discovery, wisdom, intuition, straight to the source, poetry, divination and mediation, creative energies, wisdom, understanding, inspiration, the divine sage, enlightenment.

Deities associated with Hazel

Mercury, Hermes, Thor, Mac Coll, Aengus, Artemis, Diana, Brighid.

Tree Description

The hazel is a deciduous tree native to the Northern Hemisphere and rather than having just one single trunk it tends to produce a thick mass of long arching branches. However, if left uncut, it can produce a trunk and reach a height of 8-10m. In winter it is recognizable as a mass of branches, yellowish-brown twigs with its conspicuous green, rounded buds and the immature catkins.

Hazel leaves are rounded with double-serrate margins, pointy tipped with soft prickly hair. It has both male and female flowers on the same tree, although the hazel flowers must be pollinated by pollen from other hazel trees.

Its flowers are distinctive in the spring, coming before the leaves, with single-sex male catkins, which are pale yellow and 5–8 cm long. Female catkins are very small and largely concealed in the buds, with only the bright-red, 1-to-3 mm-long styles visible.

The fruit of the hazel is the hazelnut and are found in clusters of between 1-4 nuts. 1–2.5 cm long and 1–2 cm diameter, surrounded by a husk which encloses the nut. First showing as green and then turning to brown when ripe.

Uses

The nuts of all hazels are edible. Hazel is a traditional material used for making wattle, withy fencing, baskets, and the frames of coracle boats. The wood can also be twisted or knotted, and used for thatching spars, net stakes, water divining sticks, hurdles and furniture.

The tree once coppiced, regenerates new shoots which means that there can be harvests every few years. Today, hazel coppice has become an important management strategy in the conservation of woodland habitats for wildlife. The resulting timber is used in many ways and is becoming increasingly popular as pea sticks, and bean poles used by gardeners.

Interesting Spiritual Info

The hazel tree is the tree of immortal wisdom and is linked with magic manifestation, spirit contact, protection, prosperity, divination, dowsing, dreams, wisdom-knowledge, marriage, fertility, intelligence and inspiration. The Hazel is associated with meditation and mediation.

It represents intuition, poetic skills, and the power of divination. Creative energies can be channelled to help inspire you to be a mover and shaker. Hazel is a tree that is well known to be sacred to the fairy folk and the Fey. The Salmon of Knowledge, in Celtic tradition, was said to have eaten nine nuts of poetic wisdom that had dropped into its sacred pool from the hazel tree beside it. Each nut that was eaten became a spot on the salmon's skin.

The tree itself provides, protection and shade. Fences and baskets can be made from its branches. Forked sticks are used as dowsing rods to find water or sometimes treasure. It is said that if you need magical protection whilst out and about in nature, quickly draw a circle of protection around yourself with a hazel stick. Should you wish to employ the help of certain fairies, string hazel nuts together on a cord and hang up in your house, or over your altar.

Tree Medicine

Raw hazelnuts are rich in fats, proteins, minerals and vitamins, as in vitamin E, thiamine, manganese, riboflavin, niacin, pantothenic acid, vitamin B6, folates, vitamin C, vitamin K, calcium, iron, magnesium, phosphorus, potassium, and zinc. Hazel nuts are excellent for preventing kidney stones and providing high amount of energy.

Manganese has been proven to protect against diet-induced diabetes through improving insulin secretion. The nuts are also good for protecting the heart as their fats are mainly unsaturated ones. It also contains magnesium, which is an essential mineral for the heart and maintaining a normal heartbeat.

Hazelnut's minerals and vitamins are great for the brain. Vitamin E can protect brain cells from oxidative damage caused by free radicals. Thiamine plays a key role in maintaining brain function, and its deficiency may lead to several brain disorders. The nuts contain folates or vitamin B9, whose deficiency has been linked with cognitive decline and some forms of dementia, such as Alzheimer's disease. Apart from improving brain function, folates also prevent neural tube defects such as spina bifida and anencephaly.

Hazelnuts are a rich source of antioxidants. From vitamin E, vitamin C, to manganese; these antioxidants make them a good cancer-fighting food. Vitamin E has been labelled by many as a cancer preventing supplement. Research has found it very helpful in reducing the risk for lung, prostate, colon, and breast cancer. In addition to preventing cancer, vitamin E also prevents the disintegration of red blood cells.

Vitamin E is also good for the well-being of both your skin and hair, protecting the skin against the harmful effects of ultraviolet rays and dryness. It helps fight premature aging and reduces skin inflammation. Vitamin E has also been attributed to clearing dark spots, treating scars, clearing wrinkles and fighting acne.

Hazel nut oil can be used for thread worm infections in children. Hazel trees were used by Indigenous Americans to help heal teeth issues, with tea and roots used to help heal haemorrhaging. Heart disease, indigestion, and eye issues were all health issues that were relieved with the use of all parts of the tree, including branches, bark, and roots used often in teas. When used with mead and honey it can cure a chronic cough.

Herbal Medicine: Corylus avellana

Common Name: European hazel, filbert.

Parts Used: Leaves, nuts, nut oil.

Overview: Hazel nuts are rich in phosphorus, magnesium, potassium and copper. A group of constituents called oligomeric proanthocyanidins can be extracted from the leaves. These support collagen in the body's connective tissues and can be useful in treating varicose veins and bruising. Also good for decoction for diarrhoea.

The nuts are a good source of nutrients. Hazelnut oil has a pleasant nutty aroma and taste. It is a good nourishing oil for promoting healthy skin and hair. Recent research has revealed that hazel leaves contain the anti-cancer compound taxol.

Cautions: None found.

Ogam Channel Healing Guide

Spiritual/Mind: Creativity Depression   Enlightenment   Fear and doubts Fertility Finding self-love Going straight to the heart of the matter Inspiration Intuition Letting go of fear Mediation Meditation Mental Blocks Protection Open up to creative energies Self-honesty Wisdom Unable to make decisions Understanding

Head: Alzheimer's disease   Anencephaly   Brain issues   Cognitive issues Dementia Eczema Eye issues Headaches Hair Psoriasis Scalp sensitivity Spina bifida Teeth issues

Chest: Blood   Chronic cough   Heart disease Red blood cells (disintegration)

Stomach: Constipation Diarrhoea Gastrointestinal Problems Indigestion Morning sickness Thread worm

Kidney: Kidney stones

Cancer: Breast cancer Colon cancer Lung cancer   Prostate cancer

Skin: Acne Bruising   Dark spots (skin)   Inflammations Wrinkles

Bowels: Haemorrhoids.

Arteries/Veins: Varicose veins

General: Diet induced diabetes   Haemorrhaging Nutrients Pregnancy (strength during) Premature aging

Flower Remedy

When life feels like a struggle and you are creatively stuck, you need to get in touch with your intuition. To push your boundaries and be comfortable within your abilities you need to be relaxed and happy to go with the flow.

Hazel flower essence helps you to let go of expectations and patterns of thinking that cause fear and doubts. By tuning into the things you can control, brings inner peace and calm, so allowing you to be able to explore new directions from firm foundations and to follow your intuition and inspiration.

Notes

Hazelnuts to the Celts represented both wisdom and inspiration. There are many variations on an ancient tale that told of nine hazel trees which grew around a sacred pool, each year its nuts fell into the water and were eaten by the salmon (a fish sacred to the Druids), they absorbed the wisdom. A Druid teacher, in his bid to become enlightened, caught one of these special salmon and asked his student to cook, but not to eat it. While it was cooking, a blister formed upon the fish and the pupil used his thumb to burst it, so causing some of its juices to splash over his thumb. Not being able to resist the urge, the student sucked it, and absorbed the fish's wisdom. This boy was called Fionn Mac Cumhail (Fin McCool) and went on to become one of the most heroic leaders in Gaelic mythology.

Folklore

In Grimm's Fairy Tales there is a story of the Hazel Branch which offers the greatest protection from snakes and other creepy things. Pilgrim's staffs were often made of hazel to protect them on their travels. Hazel also has a reputation as a magical tree. Its nuts were carried as charms to ward off rheumatism. In medieval times the hazel tree was a symbol of fertility.

In Greek mythology, Hermes carried a hazel staff to help him travel through the human and spirit realms. Mercury, who was Hermes's Roman equivalent, also carried a Hazel staff which gave him great wisdom.

According to the Celts, the hazel tree was at the heart of the Otherworld. There are nine magic hazel-trees which hang over the Well of Wisdom, dropping their purple nuts into the water, causing bubbles of mystical inspiration to float to the surface and travel down the flowing waters from the well. The Salmon of Knowledge and Inspiration would eat the nuts and then send the empty husks floating downstream. It is said that whoever eats these nuts or the salmon, gain great poetic and prophetic powers.

In Scotland, a hazel grove was called a *calltuin*, and various places called Calton are associated with portals to the Otherworld. Calton Hill, which is situated between Leith and Edinburgh, was still being used for magical gatherings in the 17th century. The hazel is found at many holy wells throughout Britain and Ireland, and pilgrims still tie pieces of cloth to its branches as an offering. In legend and folklore, the hazel, along with the apple and hawthorn, is a tree often found at the border between the worlds where the Fey exist.

The English word comes from the Anglo Saxon *haesl*, which originally signified a baton of authority. The hazelnut was so highly esteemed it was called the sacred food of the gods. In Anglo-Saxon England pig herders used hazel rods to drive their animals. In Norse mythology it was known as the Tree of Knowledge and was sacred to Thor.

In Ireland, the last kings of the Tuatha Dé Danaan, were MacCuill, (son of Hazel), MacCecht (Son of the Plough) and MacGréine (Son of the Sun) divided the island into three so that the country was said to be under the plough, the sun or the hazel, for 'these were the things they put above all other.' The Hill of Tara, which was the chief seat of kingship in Ireland was built near a hazel wood, and the great monastery of Clonord was established in a sacred pagan place known as The Wood of the White Hazel: Ross-Finnchuill.

Hazel has been widely used for protection against evil. Finn Mac Cool bore a hazel wood shield making him invincible in battle. Sea captains wearing a cap with hazel woven were guaranteed to weather any storm. Cattle driven through the Beltane and Midsummer bonfires had their backs singed with hazel rods to protect them against disease and the evil eye, and then the scorched rods were used to drive them for the rest of the year.

In 19th century Devon, old women traditionally greeted new brides with gifts of hazel for fertility in the same wary that rice or confetti is used today. In England, there was a link between a large show of hazel catkins and the coming of many babies. Apparently even up to the 1950s, there was a saying, 'Plenty of catkins means plenty of prams.' Traditionally on Holy Cross Day (14 September), there was a custom of children going *nutting*. It lasted up until the First World War. Forked twigs of hazel are favoured by diviners searching for water.

Apple   Quert   (Wholeness)

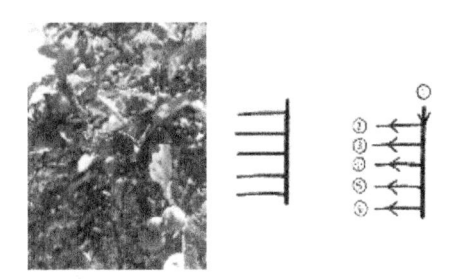

Quert corresponds to the letter Q in the Ogam alphabet and is associated with the Apple tree. This symbol represents love, choice and rebirth.

Quert pronounced: kyert

Status: Peasant-tree

Element: Water

Gender: Feminine

Powers: Quert provides choice of beauties which are yours to make.

Keywords

Health, vitality, regeneration, recovery, wholeness, integration, choice of beauty, a choice that must be made.

Deities associated with Apple

Aphrodite, Venus, Helen, Hera, Astarte, Ashtoreth, Ishtar, Cerridwen, Athene, Nemesis, Eurystheus, Olwen, Gwen, Arwen, Shekinah, Heracles, Atlas, Dionysus, Zeus, Paris and Cupid.

Tree Description

Crab apple comes more as a shrub like tree, found in hedges, woodlands and especially round oak trees. Its bark is scaly, pale brown/grey and smooth.

The leaves are rounded or more oval shaped. When opened, they are woolly but expand hairless and are held on short stubby shoots or spurs. The flowers are large and flat, coloured pink or white with 5 petals and can be up to 6cm across. They come in small clusters and appear after the leaves sometime in May. The fruit grow up to 2 cm across and become yellow when ripe. They taste sour and come on bare stalks.

Uses

There are many different species of apple bred for various tastes and use, including cooking, eating raw and cider production. Apples have religious and mythological significance in many cultures which include Greek, Norse, and European Christian traditions.

Apple fruit, cooked or raw, can be made into dozens of food and beverages, such as apple juice, apple pie, pudding, pastry, dumplings, apple cider, apple wine, butter, apple sauce, preserves and candy. Roasted spiced apples are a favorite Christmastime treat. Crab apples (a small, sour apple) are popular with jelly and jam makers.

Apple tree wood chips are used for the barbecue, using the limbs, twigs or stump. Apple chips can also be used in smoking, hot or cold meats etc. Apple wood chips are used as a nutrient rich feeder for the garden, used as mulch and used for aesthetic value when lining pathways or garden borders.

Pruned limbs or branches are used as support stakes for young garden plants. Apples are used in many cosmetic lotions, shampoos, and cellulite products. Apple cider vinegar is known to clean hair, specifically oily hair. This vinegar works as a skin tonic as well, improving blood circulation. With a combination of enzymes, antioxidants, vitamins A, B and C, beta carotene and a wealth of others, cider vinegar naturally balances the skin's PH. Apple tree wood is also used to create furniture.

Interesting Spiritual Information

The Apple is associated with choice. It might be between similar attractive things and extremely hard to choose, but if a choice is taken it will see you right. In Norse myth, Idunna was charged with keeping the 'apples of immortality' ripe and ready for the Gods. The fruit helped keep the Gods young. Useful for love and healing magic concerned with choice.

Tree Medicine

Apples contain sugars, amino acids, magnesium, iron, potassium, carbohydrates, vitamins C, B and B2, phosphates, tartaric acids, pectin, and mineral salts. They are prescribed for intestinal infections, constipation, mental and physical fatigue, hypertension, rheumatism, gout, anemia, bronchitis, urine retention, hepatic disorders, gastric and kidney malfunctions, hoarseness, coughing, and excess cholesterol in the blood.

Apple cider vinegar eases allergies which helps relieve sinus infections, acid reflux, sore throats, acne, high cholesterol, arthritis, sunburn, eczema, warts and gout. Apples contain a list of phytonutrients that function as antioxidants and support heart health, including catechin, phloridzin and chlorogenic acid. Apples also have anti-fungal and antiseptic properties.

Crushed apple pulp will heal inflammation or small flesh wounds with application.

Tree bark is used to treat fevers and diarrhoea. Stewed apples can be used as a laxative.

Baked apples are great as a warm poultice for fevers and sore throat.

Apples contain chemicals that can affect cancer cells (lung cancer), diabetes, dysentery, fever, heart problems, warts, scurvy, alzheimer's, Good for improving muscle strength. Good for metabolism. Stimulates the Liver & Kidney. Nervous System Tonic.

Warning: Do not eat cooked or raw apples in the evening, as they may start to ferment in the stomach overnight.

Herbal Medicine: Malus species

Common names: Apple, crab apple.

Parts Used: Bark, fruit, apple cider, apple cider vinegar.

Overview: Chewing raw apples is great exercise for the teeth and gums with the fruit's acids helping in cleaning the teeth. They also help clean the liver, help cure constipation by causing normal bowel movements, and their soluble fibre content can help lower cholesterol levels so protecting the heart and circulation.

When baked they can be applied as a warm poultice to sore throats and skin inflammations.

Cooked, the apple works as a laxative. Strangely, the raw peel helps with diarrhoea.

As a cider it corrects intestinal flora, reduces stomach acidity, corrects gas and aids the kidneys in their work; take 3-4 cups a day.

Apple cider vinegar and water make a rinse to help restore hair, help the scalp and skin. Use equal parts of vinegar and water, blondes should use white vinegar.

For help with digestion, use apple cider vinegar, water and honey when eating meals; use 2 teaspoons of vinegar to a glass, the honey is to help with the taste.

Cautions: Excessive fruit consumption can cause griping abdominal pains and diarrhoea. Crab apples can specifically cause these symptoms so should not be eaten raw.

How does it work?

Apples contain pectin, which helps bulk up the stool to treat diarrhoea and constipation. Apples also contain some chemicals that seem to be able to kill bacteria, reduce swelling in the body, and kill cancer cells. Apple peel contains a chemical called ursolic acid that is suspected to have a role in building muscle and metabolism.

Apples are used to control diarrhoea or constipation, and for the softening, passage, and collection of gallstones. They are also used to prevent cancer, especially lung cancer. Other uses include treating cancer, diabetes, dysentery, fever, heart problems, warts, and a vitamin C-deficiency condition called scurvy. Some people also use apples for weight loss and cleaning their teeth. It is also used for Alzheimer's disease and improving muscle strength.

Apple is applied to the head for baldness.

Ogam Channel Healing Guide

Spiritual/Mind: Anxiety and stress Choice Depression Despondency Fear based issues Fussiness Integrating Keeping good health Integration Negative impressions Linking in with the Goddess Obsession Recovery Open to self-love Prosperity Regeneration Relaxing Vitality Self-dislike Wholeness

Head/Neck: Acne Alzheimer's Eczema Hangover Hoarseness Hypertension Mental and physical fatigue Nervous System Sinus Infection Sore throat

Chest: Anemia Bronchitis Blood production Cholesterol Diabetes Fevers Excess cholesterol in the blood Heart problems Metabolism

Liver: Liver

Urinary: Hepatic disorders Kidney Urine retention

Stomach: Acid reflux Diarrhoea Digestion Constipation Fasting (Aid) Gastric malfunctions

Sex: Fertility

Skin: Small flesh wounds Sunburn Warts

Muscle: Muscle strength

Joints: Arthritis Rheumatism

Cancer: Cancer cells (lung cancer)

General: Dysentery Gout Scurvy Strengthens whole metabolism

Flower Remedy

When you are suffering from self-dislike, despondency,

obsessions, fussiness, and anxiety, apples act to strengthen the whole metabolism. It balances the digestion, stimulates blood production as well as helping to cleanse the system. It also has diuretic, febrifugal and relaxing properties, and stimulates the appetite.

The crab apple can also be used directly externally, thus acting on the mental and physical levels as well. Crab apple will remove negative impression, for example after an unpleasant task. 10 drops can be added to a full bath, 5 drops are enough for a compress. Practitioners have recommended crab apple when fasting, and even to overcome the effects of a hangover (4 drops every half hour). If an open wound is infected, you should use it to draw the poison out.

Notes

Celts saw the apple as a symbol of creativity and as an emblem of art and poetry. The meaning of apple trees is also associated with virtue, and both the tree and fruit are symbols of purity and motherhood. By looking at the apple tree trunk formation, they saw females in various poses and considered the tree as a beacon of fertility. Apple wood was often burned during fertility rites and festivals carried out in the winter months. These were demonstrations to beckon bountiful abundance upon the return of spring as well as symbolically insure continuation of large, healthy families.

Folklore

Unfortunately, the word *apple* was used as a generic term for all fruit, other than berries, including nuts, as late as the 17th century.

In Greek myth, Aphrodite (Venus in Roman myth), was the supreme goddess of beauty and love. She won the battle between herself, Hera and Athene to be called the most beautiful, by Paris, who gave her an apple to mark this decision. Paris and Helen (of Troy) set up many shrines in recognition of Aphrodite and so the apple became known as the source of beauty, love and wisdom. Mother Gaia gave a wedding gift of a sacred apple tree to Hera when she married Zeus.

An epigram by Plato states: 'I throw the apple at you, and if you are willing to love me, take it and share your girlhood with me; but if your thoughts are what I pray they are not, even then take it, and consider how short-lived is beauty.'

Apples have a long history of being used for divination, to foretell the future in matters of love and prosperity. These rituals as well as many others were performed at Samhain, as the apple is linked to the Celtic Otherworld and the tree is seen to possess magical properties. Samhain is the time of the year when the veil between the worlds is at its thinnest. It presents itself as a portal between the physical world and that of spirit. It is also seen as an ideal time to undertake shamanic journeys, consult with the dead and spirit realms, to gain oracular knowledge and use healing energy. If you cut the apple sideways, you will find the shape of the pentagram from the formation of its pips. It is an ancient symbol of knowledge and sacred to the Celtic death Goddess, Cailleach, the Crone, the Veiled One, and Samhain is her time of year.

According to Druidic law, the essence of sacred apples was the three drops of liquid which escaped from Cerridwen's cauldron and had originally descended from heaven into the cauldron. Symbolically, from these drops rose three streams which corresponds to the three pillars of the Druidic tree of life. These rays represent male and female and their united expression. These rays also correspond to the Druid's holy symbol, the three rays of light, vision symbols and the understanding of the first two. From these rays all art was born and is called the Awen. In Celtic times, apples were thought of as the food of the gods and apple trees were blessed by Druids to make sure the crops were good and wholesome.

In Norse mythology, the goddess Iounn was the provider of apples to the Gods. These apples helped give them eternal youth.

Apples appear in many religions, as a mystical or forbidden fruit. Adam and Eve, both took a bite of the forbidden apple of knowledge which saw them being thrown out of the Garden of Eden.

Early Saxon sympathetic magic depended upon associations. You were encouraged to write a holy name on an apple and eat it on three consecutive days to cure a fever. The apple was considered extremely effective against venom, or poison, a purifier and cleanser, all of which corresponds with the apple's well-known properties today.

Our folk memory is rich with such phrases as; "an apple a day keeps the doctor away," for good reason. The malic and tartaric acids of the apple particularly benefit people of sedentary habits as they neutralise the acid products of indigestion. It is a very digestible fruit; an excellent baby food and it aids the digestion of other foods. In traditional herbal treatment, crab apple is used for cleansing and as a de-toxicant for both internal and external wounds. It helps to heal skin tissue, is anti-inflammatory and anti-septic, hence the connection in our folklore with beauty. A poultice made from the boiled or roasted fruit will remove burn marks from the skin. The same boiled fruit is good for sore or inflamed eyes.

There are old folk remedies for curing rheumatism by rubbing the affected area with a rotten apple, and a cure for warts by rubbing the warts with two halves of an apple and then burying it. Interestingly, the pectin in the apple acts as a germicide, promoting new skin growth and thus providing a medical basis for the old wives' tale.

12

Vine Muin (Harvest)

Muin corresponds to the letter M in the Ogam alphabet and is associated with the Vine. This symbol represents prophecy, truth and inner development.

Muin pronounced: Mwin

Status: Chieftain-tree

Element: Fire (Blackberry: Water)

Gender: Masculine (Blackberry: Feminine)

Celtic Tenth Month: August

Powers: Muin is prophecy and inspiration.

Keywords

Harvest, festivity, celebration, successful completion, Alban Elfed, inner development, prophecy, ability to roam widely and gather.

Deities associated with Vine

Dionysus, Bacchus, Hathor.

Tree Description

Vine is any plant with a growth habit of trailing or climbing stems, liannas or runners. *Vine* usually applies exclusively to grapevines, while the term *climber* is used for all climbing plants. Grapes are a type of fruit that grow in clusters of 15 to 300, and can be crimson, black, dark blue, yellow, green, orange, and pink. White grapes are green in colour and are evolutionarily derived from the purple grape. Grapes are typically an ellipsoid shape resembling a prolate sphere.

Uses

Grapes which have been commercially cultivated are usually classified as table or wine grapes. They are either eaten raw or used to make wine. In most of Europe and North America, dried grapes are referred to as raisins. A currant is a dried Zante Black Corinth grape. A *sultana* was originally a raisin made from Sultana grapes of Turkish origin. Grape juice is obtained from crushing and blending grapes into a liquid. The juice is often sold in shops or made into wine, brandy or vinegar.

Interesting Spiritual Information

The release of prophetic powers. Using wine to dissolve the inhibitions allows you to speak with more perception and truth than you might normally. There are times when we need to let our logical and intellectual capacities go so that we can pull in our other resources and let subtle intuition surface and have its say.

The Druids classified anything with a woody stalk as a tree, and so therefore vine is listed among the sacred Ogam ranks. From the Druid perspective, the vine earned its symbolism from its opportunistic ability to dig in wherever possible and gain a strong foothold to assure its own growth. There is a very powerful message of *going with the flow*. The thorns of these vines are symbolic of protecting oneself when necessary.

Lastly, the Celts also recognized the vine's predominant growth formation is in the shape of a spiral, a sacred symbol for: consciousness, development, renewal and growth.

Tree Medicine

The leaves of the vine when gathered in June contain a mixture of cane sugar and glucose, tartaric acid, potassium bi-tartrate, quercetine, quercitrin, tannin, amidon, malic acid, gum, inosite, an uncrystallizable fermentable sugar and oxalate of calcium; when gathered in the autumn they contain much more quercetine and less trace of quercitrin.

The ripe fruit juice called *must*, contains sugar, gum, malic acid, potassium bi-tartrate and inorganic salts, when fermented this forms the wine of commerce. The dried ripe fruit commonly called raisins, contain dextrose and potassium acid tartrate.

Grape sugar is rapid in increasing strength and repairing waste in fevers but is unsuitable for inflammatory or gouty conditions.

The juice of the unripe fruit, 'Verjuice,' contains malic, citric, tartaric, racemic and tannic acids, potassium bi-tartrate, sulphate of potash and lime. The seeds contain tannin and a fixed oil. The seeds and leaves are astringent, the leaves being formerly used to stop haemorrhages and bleeding. They are used dried and powdered as a cure for dysentery in cattle. Seeds contain antioxidant compounds and extracts are sold commercially. Grape seed extract has been positively tested for use in treating microcirculatory disorders such as varicose veins.

The sap forms an excellent lotion for weak eyes and specks on the cornea. In cases of anaemia and a state of exhaustion the restorative power of grapes is excellent, especially when taken with a light, but nourishing diet.

In cases of small-pox, grapes have proved useful owing to their bi-tartrate of potash content; they are also said to be of benefit in cases of neuralgia, sleeplessness, etc.

Dried grapes: the raisins of commerce, are largely used in the manufacture of galencials, the seeds being separated and rejected as they give a very bitter taste. Raisins are demulcent, nutritive and slightly laxative.

Leaf tea is used to treat diarrhoea, hepatitis, thrush and stomach-ache. Leaf poultice applied externally for sore chest, headache, rheumatism, and fevers. Red wine in moderation can be of benefit to the heart and circulation.

Ogam Channel Healing Guide

Spiritual/Mind: Ability to roam widely and gather   Celebration   Conscious development   Divine inspiration   Energising   Festivity   Fun/levity   Inner spiritual development   Increase the positive self   Persistence-bears fruit   Positivity   Prophecy   Renewal and Growth   Self-love   Successful completion of project   Wise-ness

Head: Eyesight   Fevers   Headache   Neuralgia   Sleeplessness

Chest: Anaemia   Circulation   Heart   Hepatitis   Sore chest

Bowels: Diarrhoea

Joints: Rheumatism

Arterial/Veins: Varicose veins

Genital: Thrush

General: Exhaustion   Stopping bleeding   Smallpox

Flower Remedy

When one is so sure of their own mind, they start telling people what is best for them, Vine is an ideal remedy to help bring out their more positive selves. Instead of trying to instill fear into others, issuing orders and expecting instant responses, they will become wiser, gentler and more loving in their approach. It helps to show people their positive sides.

Notes

Spiritual self-cultivation is the underlying theme behind the rites of harvest as they bring divine inspiration and ecstasy. Alcoholic festival celebrations were a metaphor in the ancient world for achieving higher states of consciousness, attained through singing, dancing and festivals. Shamans today, drum, chant and sing scared power songs to take one into an altered state.

Folklore

According to Greek mythology, Dionysus is the god of nature and the god of wine and inspiration. He was known as the god of ecstasy and his cult was one of the mystery religions. It was Dionysus who first produced wine from the fruit of the vine and taught how to tend for the grapes properly. His nature mirrored the nature of wine as he could bring great joy and ecstasy on one hand, and terrible rage and brutality on the other. He was associated with death and rebirth. As Dionysus wandered the world he was accompanied by his Maenads, who were wild women, often drunk on wine and encouraged all they met to worship him. They dressed in fawn skins and carried hazel wands, tipped with pinecones.

There were never any temples erected to Dionysus, as they worshipped in the woods.

When Dionysus is usually depicted, he wears a crown of ivy and covered in vine leaves and grape, an image like the Green Man.

Ivy   Gort   (Tenacity)

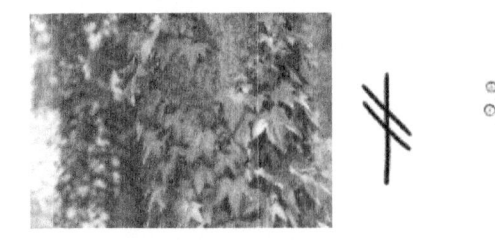

Gort corresponds to the letter G in the Ogam alphabet and is associated with the Ivy. This symbol represents tenacity, growth and both physical and spiritual development.

Gort pronounced: Gohrd

Status: Chieftain-tree

Element: Water

Gender: Feminine

Celtic Eleventh Month: September

Powers: Gort is the spiral search for self.

Keywords

Tenacity, ruthlessness, achievement, restriction, the second harvest, spiral of the self, inner searching, soul search or you will take a wrong turn, development, transformation.

Deities associated with Ivy

Bacchus, Dionysus, Osiris, Isis, Ariadne, Arianrhod, Cerridwen, Gorgopa, Hymen, Lakshmi, Kundalini, Persephone, Saturn, the White Goddess.

Tree Description

Ivy is an evergreen climbing or ground-creeping woody-plant, native to western, central and southern Europe. On level ground they remain creeping, but on suitable surfaces for climbing, including trees, rocky outcrops or man-made structures such as buildings, they can climb to at least 30m above the ground.

There are two leaf types; juvenile shoots, which are slender, flexible and scrambling or climbing with small aerial roots to fix itself to the host structure, and adult shoots, being thicker, self-supporting and without roots. The flowers are greenish yellow with 5 small petals. Produced in imbels in autumn to early winter and are very rich in nectar.

The fruit is a greenish-black, dark purple or yellow berry, with 1 to 5 seeds, which ripen in late winter to mid-spring. The seeds are usually dispersed by birds which eat the berries. Species of ivy can be distinguished by the different shape and size of the leaves, the structure of the leaf trichomes and the size and colour of the flowers and fruit.

Uses

Ivy is used for planting in small planting spaces, on tall or wide walls for aesthetic reasons, or to hide horrible sights such as walls and fences. They have varied horticultural uses depending on their foliage and unusual leaf shapes. There are reports that ivy used to be made into a potent ale and was used with hallucinogenic mushrooms to create states of frenzy. Some sources inform that ivy can remove a drunken state.

Interesting Spiritual Information

The ivy symbolizes the maze of the labyrinth. It is the spiral of the self in the search for its self. It is the wandering of the soul, circling inwards and outwards, seeking nourishment and experience in a bid to achieving its goal of enlightenment.

Tree Medicine

One of the best-known benefits of ivy, and in particular, English Ivy, is for inflammation issues in the body. If you suffer from arthritis, gout or rheumatism, you can either take it in tea form or apply the leaves directly to the spot of inflammation.

For people who experience discomfort and pain from an injury or surgery, topical application is recommended. This can heal internal inflammation as well, which has a variety of other applications in various bodily systems.

Studies have shown a link between liver and gallbladder function and the use of ivy leaves, helping organs function better to release toxins from the body and purifying the blood.

It also relieves the discomfort and irritation of psoriasis, eczema, acne, and other skin-related conditions.

For centuries, people have used ivy leaves to minimize the pain and infection of burning wounds including open sores/wounds on the skin. There are additional antibacterial properties, in addition to the protective nature of the saponins, which help prevent spasms and eliminate congestion by breaking up the phlegm and mucus in the bronchial system. It is also an effective remedy for allergic reactions and asthma, as they reduce the inflammation of those passages.

Although research is still ongoing, ivy leaves properties have suggested significant antioxidant activity, and may have the ability to prevent the spread or development of cancer.

By eliminating free radicals and preventing mutation and apoptosis, they might help protect the body from a wide range of chronic diseases, including cancer.

Ivy has anthelmintic and anti-parasitic qualities, ideal for elimination intestinal worms and lice. Traditional folk medicine used English ivy internally for liver, spleen and gallbladder disorders, gout, arthritis, rheumatism and dysentery. Eternally it was used for burns, calluses, cellulitis, inflammations, neuralgia, parasitic disorders, ulcers, rheumatic complaints and phlebitis.

Folk medicine used ivy leaf poultices externally as a treatment for swollen glands and chronic leg ulcers and topical decoctions have been used as a natural treatment for scabies, lice and sunburn. Also seen to be good for asthma, bronchitis, colds, chronic pulmonary disorders, sore throats and getting rid of stretch marks!

Warning: Be aware that ivy contains a poisonous substance called Hederin. The leaves and berries are said to be cathartic, diaphoretic and stimulant. Some people have reported that direct contact with the skin results in irritation, so if you have sensitive skin, apply it moderately at first and see your reaction.

Herbal Medicine: Hedera Helix

Plant Family: Hedera.

Parts Used: Twig and leaf.

Overview: Tender Ivy twigs can help deal with sunburn, simmer them in salves.

The leaves can be used as a douche for vaginal infections.

To help heal nerves, sinews, ulcers, enlarged glands, boils and abscesses create a poultice and place on affected area. Ground ivy is good for: solution to clean the eyes, teas to help nervousness and ulcers. A decoction of the plant is used to treat skin diseases.

Ogam Channel Healing Guide

Spiritual/Mind: Acknowledging achievements   Compassion   Courage   Development   Emotional trauma   Fear   Fidelity   Good Luck   Inner soul searching   Intelligence   Love   Loyalty

Nervousness   Looking for safe transformation   Power rebalance   Resilience   Ruthlessness   Self-love   Survival   Stability to the mind-body system   Tenacity   Toughness   Transformation

Head/Neck: Eyes Fear Neuralgia Shock   Sore throats

Chest: Asthma   Bronchitis   Colds   Pulmonary Disorders   Purifying blood

Glands: Swollen glands

Stomach: Dysentery Intestinal worms

Organs: Liver   Gall bladder   Spleen

Skin: Acne Burn wounds Calluses Eczema Lice   Psoriasis Scabies Skin diseases Sun burn Stretch marks

Genitals: Vaginal infections

Skin: Inflammations Leg ulcers Cellulitis

Joints: Arthritis   Rheumatism

Cancer: Cancer

General: Ulcers   Gout

Flower Remedy

When having experienced a terrible shock, or emotional trauma and even an experience that makes us question whether we want to live or die, Ivy can help us to put down solid roots and ground us back into the real world. Ivy mirrors the properties that we are looking for. It can awaken in us its powers of toughness, resilience and power. Note that Ivy is a survivor! It brings vital stability to the mind-body system, giving it time to rebalance and adjust to the new situation.

Notes

Ivy was believed to be very powerful by the Druids, more powerful than its enemy, the vine and quite sinister. In old Ireland, when growing on or near a house, ivy was thought to protect it from evil. However, if it died or fell down, then hard luck would befall those within.

Ivy is also associated with good luck and fertility. At Yuletide it was believed to bring peace to the household. Ivy was also linked to inspiration and often worn by poets in the form of a crown.

Folklore

In Egypt, Isis searched for parts of her dead husband, Osiris, which had been cut up and placed in many hidden places. Once she had located them all, he was restored, and became a reborn god, staying in the Underworld. It is in this story that we see the association with ivy as a plant of life, death, renewal and also equated with fertility.

Ivy was dedicated to the Greek god Dionysus, the god of intoxication. He is often seen with a wreath of ivy on his head and holding a wand, entwined with ivy and vine leaves.

Ivy leaves were thought to prevent intoxication and the act of binding the brow with ivy was seen as a counterbalance to the vine. The negative effects of drinking too much wine could be removed by a handful of ivy leaves, gently bruised and boiled in wine and drank. In Ancient Greece wreaths of ivy were used to crown victorious athletes. There was also the tradition of priests giving ivy to newlyweds, as a symbol of fidelity.

In Ancient Rome, Bacchus, god of intoxication, wore a wreath of ivy as it was thought it could prevent a person from becoming drunk (see above). Traditionally pubs and taverns in the UK have used painted signs depicting ivy bushes or ivy-wrapped poles to advertise themselves, many pubs are still called The Ivy. The clinging nature of ivy makes it an ideal symbol of love and friendship.

The plant was sacred to the Druids and considered the female counterpart to the masculine holly. In medieval Christian symbolism, because ivy can cling to dead trees and remains green, it was also seen as a symbol of the eternal life of the soul after the death of the body.

In the British Christmas Carol, *The Holly and the Ivy*, the ivy represents a symbol for the Virgin Mary. Together with mistletoe and holly, ivy is a traditional herb used to decorate houses for the Christmas season. During the Romantic Movement in landscape painting, ivy covered ruins became a standard symbol for the evanescence of human endeavor and the sublime power of nature. Ivy's qualities are known as, compassion, loyalty, resilience and intelligence. English ivy is a member of the ginseng family and has been used in traditional herbal medicine both in Europe and Asia since ancient times. Historically, English ivy leaves formed the poet's crown.

Reed Ngetal (Direct action)

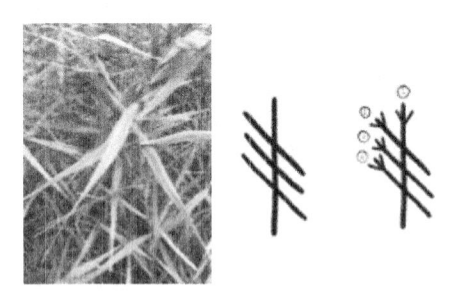

Ngetal corresponds to the letter Ng in the Ogam alphabet and is associated with the Reed. This symbol represents direct action, healing and communication.

NGetal pronounced: NYAY-tuhl

144

Status: shrub

Element: Earth

Gender: Changeable

Celtic Twelfth Month: October

Powers: Reed represents direct action.

Keywords

Tree of scribes, direct action, direction of purpose, growth and meanings to the purpose of your journey, communication, knowledge, order, healing, will, protection.

Deities associated with Reed

Ningikuga, *Lady of the Pure Reed*, in Sumerian mythology was a goddess of reeds and marshes. The Goddess, Brighid, Rhiannon, Manannan, Mac Lir, Poseidon, Coventina, Pwyll.

Tree Description

Reed is a giant grass which is up to 2m tall and thin, growing at the side of rivers and streams and marshy areas. The stems are tough, stiff and last throughout the winter. It has tough rooting stems which form tangled networks in the mud/soil which can help strengthen the bank it grows on. The bark tends to remain all throughout the winter, but the vertical stems only live for one year.

They die in autumn and are replaced by its new green shoots in the spring. Their leaves are smooth, long, flat, grey-green and their sheaths surround the stem and overlap. They are about 30mm wide, are stiff and have no ligules. The flower is large and soft, it appears between August to October. It is upright but can droop as the seeds ripen. Individual spikelets are purplish or brownish with soft, white hairs surrounding each floret. The fruit are its purple-black seeds.

Uses

Reeds were used for thatching roofs and was grown expressly for that as a crop. Reed binds the soil on riverbanks. The runners are nutritious as they have mush sugar within and so are used as fodder for cattle. It is also used in spinning, by weavers. It is made into paper in Wales.

The physician would use the reed as a straw to blow powdered herbs onto the back of the throat of a sick person, and it has medicinal uses in its own right. Reed has served as a floor covering, roofing, and room deodorizer. The powdered root was used as an insecticide against fleas. Soaked in fat the stalks made a cheap alternative to candles. Reed is used in wood-wind instruments and also for pens and arrows.

Interesting Spiritual Information

With reed, you have the ability of finding order whilst all around you others see chaos. With this ability comes the skills of choosing the right direction for your target and keeping the intention pure will make sure you follow the path, whatever comes your way. Reed gives you the spiritual capacity to create the spiritual weapons you will need to keep on keeping on.

The Celts had a number of symbolic meanings for the reed; purpose, protection as in an insulator, roofing material; purification - as laid out pressed reeds as flooring in their homes to deodorize and cleanse; communication - reeds made fine whistles, flutes or recorders which were highly valued particularly by the bards.

Reeds also made good candles and were viewed as beacons of light during dark nights. But reeds are also linked strongly with medicine and healing, especially to administer medicines. The Celtic Goddess most associated with the reed is the great goddess

Brighid. She is a triple goddess. Her spheres of influence are poetry, smithcraft and healing. Patroness of Druids and most especially bards, but also especially associated with healing wells and springs. Brighid's Crosses are equal armed crosses and are traditionally made from reeds.

Reed is used in spell work & ritual magic for expanded awareness, journeys to other realms, soul retrieval, harmony rituals, protection for home and balancing energy.

Tree Medicine

People take reed herb tea for digestion problems, diabetes, leukaemia, and breast cancer. Reed herb has been used directly on the skin to treat insect bites.

Reed herb is a plant. The stem and underground stem (rhizome) are used as medicine.

People take reed herb tea for digestion problems, diabetes, leukaemia, and breast cancer.

Some people put reed herb directly on the skin to treat insect bites.

How does it work?

The leaves are used in the treatment of bronchitis and cholera, the ash of the leaves is applied to nasty sores. A decoction of the flowers is used in the treatment of cholera and food poisoning. The ashes are styptic. The stem is antidote, antiemetic, antipyretic and refrigerant.

The root is antiasthmatic, antiemetic, antipyretic, antitussive, depurative, diuretic, febrifuge, lithontripic, sedative, sialogogue and stomachic. Taken internally for the treatment of diarrhoea, fevers, vomiting, coughs with thick dark phlegm, lung abscesses, urinary tract infections and food poisoning (especially from sea foods). Externally, it is mixed with gypsum and used to treat halitosis and toothache. The root is harvested in the autumn and juiced or dried for use in decoctions.

Medicinally the plant was used to treat eye problems.

Ogam Channel Healing Guide

Spiritual/Mind: Balancing energies   Bringing order into your life   Bringing out your leader abilities   Communication   Courage   Coping with hard times   Direction of purpose   For scribing   Growth   Harmony   Healing   Knowledge   Looking for direct action   Meaning to your journey   Order   Pointing you forward to your goal   Protection   Opening communication   Protection in harsh times   Will

Head: Eyes Halitosis   Toothache

Chest: Asthma   Breast cancer   Bronchitis   Cholera   Coughs   Fevers   Leukaemia   Lung abscesses

Stomach: Digestive problems   Poisoning (food- sea food)   Vomiting

Bladder: Urinary tract

Bowels: Diarrhoea

Skin: Insect bites

General: Diabetes

Flower Remedy

When the storm of life is knocking at your door, trying to bend you to its will, reed flower remedy brings you the flexibility to be able to cope with these heavy winds. It helps you stay on your personal pathway, allowing you to see what is actually happening about you and support you in your own ideas, feelings and truth.

Notes

Reed is a symbol of royalty, the tallest of grasses and is almost always associated with being close to water. Its tradition is as the word of authority – as papyrus was made from reeds. A broken reed is a broken promise.

Folklore

Known as a protector as it was used as thatch in roofing and for making talismans and charms to protect the wearer from evil. Mats were also made that smelled sweet and was associated with cleansing the home.

Knowledge, scholarship and wisdom is linked with reeds as the Druids apparently used it as paper and for writing implements. It was associated with death (arrows) and healing, as traditionally, healers used the reed as a means of blowing medicine into mouths of patients.

Reed represented the dates of Oct 28th – Nov 24th in the Celtic calendar and the time of Samhain, and All Souls Day, when the door to the other world dissolved and the dead could join their living ancestors.

Reed is also associated with Brighid, Goddess of poetry, healing and smith craft. Her crosses were woven from reed and hung for protection within the home against fire and evil spirits. They are still made today for St Brigid.

Reed flutes were a subject of legend; it is rumoured that the Pied Piper's magical flute was made of reed, and Pan's flute may also have been made from it.

Blackthorn   Straif   (Wounding)

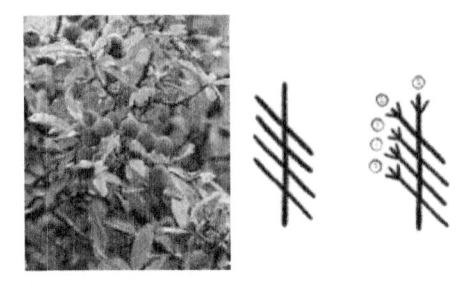

Straif corresponds to the letter S in the Ogam alphabet and is associated with the Blackthorn tree. This symbol represents authority, control and power.

Straif pronounced: Srayf

Status: Chieftain-tree

Element: Fire

Gender: Masculine

Powers: Staif is about obeying outside influences (fate) upon your life, no choice in the matter.

Keywords

Punishment, strife, pain, wounding, no choice, cleansing, fate, outside influences, resentment, confusion, refusing to see the truth, control, coercion, force, power in visible and invisible worlds.

Deities associated with Blackthorn

Crone aspect of the triple goddess, Morrigan, Cailleach, Cerridwen, Morgan le Fay, Donn, Dagda.

Tree Description

Blackthorn is a deciduous tree often found in hedgerows, in thickets or as a shrub up to 5m in height. Its bark is blackish and dense, with stiff, spiny branches and twigs twisting out in all directions. Under the bark it is bright orange and scaly with brown coloured heartwood. The tree has wicked long sharp thorns, which can turn septic if pricked.

The leaves are dark green oval shaped, with a serrated margin and turn yellow before falling off in winter leaving a twisted black skeleton. The flowers have five delicate creamy-white oval petals with red tipped stamens, clustered into a star shape in early spring. Its blossoms, are thin and rounded with toothed edges, appear before the leaves in early March, and can bloom for several months.

The fruit are black sloes, with a purple-blue waxy bloom, which ripen in autumn after the first frosts. Sloes are thin fleshed, having a strong astringent flavour when eaten fresh.

Uses

The shrub is used to make cattle-proof hedging. The wood is used for tool handles and canes and looks great when a fine polish is added. Straight blackthorn stems have traditionally been made into walking sticks or clubs, as in the shillelagh in Ireland. In the British Army, blackthorn sticks are carried by commissioned officers of the Royal Irish Regiment.

The fruit is like a small damson or plum and used for preserves, chutney and sometimes used in fruit pies, but is a little tart and astringent unless picked after the first few days of autumn frost.

A liqueur, known as sloe gin, is made by infusing gin with sloes and sugar. Vodka can also be infused with these sloes and wine can be made from fermented sloes. Sloe berry juice can be used for ink or a strong red dye for linen that washes out to a durable pale blue.

When the 5,300-year-old human mummy was discovered in 1991 in the Otzal Alps along the Austrian-Italian border, sloes were found amongst the stomach contents.

A *sloe-thorn worm* used as fishing bait is mentioned in the 15th-century work, *The Treatyse of Fishing with an Angle*, by Juliana Berners.

Blackthorn is excellent firewood and burns slowly with a good heat and little smoke. It also has medicinal uses.

Interesting Spiritual Information

Blackthorn is a winter tree and is used for purification, protection and ridding the atmosphere of negative energy. It helps with combating fear, depression and anger, it is very much associated with personal inner work, assessment, grounding and protection. Blackthorn also represents the strong action of fate or other outside influences in life. Its thorns have been used in magic, especially to pierce wax images.

Tree Medicine

The sloe berries contain the following compounds: flavonoids, tannins, glycoside, prunasin, benz aldehyde. Its pulp has been used as a face mask to help with the glow and flexibility of the skin due to it containing vitamin C and tannins. Mixing sloe berry powder with water can have a calming effect on nerves, can remove fatigue and bring vitality back to the body. The fruit is very astringent and makes a good purgative.

Flowers (gathered in April and May) are good for sore mouths, tonsils and reduce swelling in mouth and throat when made into a gargle. They have astringent, antioxidant, diaphoretic (inducing perspiration), depurative (removal of impurities in the blood), febrifuge (reducing fever), laxative, stomachic issues such as constipation and diarrhea, and diuretic properties. It also helps in the prevention of gout and rheumatism. The flowers are also taken to treat colds, breathing conditions, cough, fluid retention, general exhaustion, upset stomach, kidney stones and bladder problems, and constipation; and to treat and prevent stomach spasms. They can be used in the form of infusions for their laxative, diuretic and anti-inflammatory effects.

According to research at the University of Lódz in Poland, the presence of the flavonoid glycoside quercetin has been located in the flowers, which has anti-inflammatory properties, as well as kaempferol, another flavonoid that in preclinical studies been found to be beneficial in reducing the risk of cancers and cardiovascular disease.

The leaves are like tea leaves and are used as an adulterant of tea. Herbal tea from the leaves are known to be good for stimulating appetite.

Bark extracts have astringent properties owing to their high tannin content.

Ogam Channel Healing Guide

Spiritual/Mind: Accepting-karma   Assessment   Control   Confusion   Cleansing   Bringing you power in the visible and invisible worlds   Bringing back self-control of your life   Cleansing-resentment   Dealing with spiritual, mental and emotional wounds   Despair and despondency   Depression   Fate   Grounding   Helping in seeing the truth of the matter   Pain   Personal inner work   Protection   Protection from outside influences   Purification of mind, body and spirit   Refusing to see truth   Resentment   Suicidal thoughts   Strife

Head/Neck: Anger issues   Depression   Grounding   Mental-Health   Nerves/ fatigue   Sore mouths/ tonsils/ throat

Chest: Breathing conditions   Colds   Cough   Fluid Retention   Heart disease   Removing impurities from blood

Stomach: Constipation   Diarrhoea   Stimulating appetite

Urinary: Bladder   Kidney stones

Skin: Skin issues

Joints: Rheumatism

Cancer: Cancer

General: Gout

Flower Remedy

Blackthorn is there for the dark times when self-destruction is close to hand. Nothing seems to be going right and all our dreams have been destroyed by outside influences. Your ego might have fuelled these events through selfish thoughts or strongly held beliefs. Thoughts of suicide may come to mind as we cannot face the consequences of the perceived truth.

Blackthorn can aid in facilitating the changes needed to help us accept the challenges facing us and acknowledge that there is another way forward. Fear is stopping us seeing and moving towards the light. By illuminating our way forward, Blackthorn can help ease the pain of change, so we can develop a positive way of life.

Notes

Blackthorn was traditionally considered a sibling tree to the hawthorn and is not a particularly approachable tree as it is associated with the North wind and cold winter. The Irish believed it was protected by the Lunantishee – roguish fairies. A blackthorn rod, or wand, is used for shape shifting magic, and is believed to confer the ability to bring about change.

Folklore

Blackthorn is portrayed as an ill-omened tree in many fairy tales throughout Europe. Called Straif in the Ogam, it has an ominous reputation in the Celtic tree lore. The English word 'strife' is said to derive from this Celtic word. A long hard winter is referred to as a Blackthorn Winter.

To witches, it often represents the dark side of the Craft. Known as a sacred tree to the Crone aspect of the Triple Goddess, it represents the Waning and Dark Moons. Blackthorn is the keeper of dark secrets. The tree is linked with warfare, wounding and death, associated with the Scottish Cailleach - the Crone of Death, and the Irish Morrigan. In Scotland, the winter begins when the Cailleach *also the Goddess of Winter* strikes the ground with her staff made of blackthorn.

According to Christian folklore, blackthorn is seen as a sinister tree as it is associated with witches. Blackthorn was often used for 'binding and blasting.' A black rod is a blackthorn wand with fixed thorns on one end, used to cause harm to others. In British folklore, witches use blackthorn thorns to pierce poppets in their curses, called the 'pins of slumber.' In South Devon, witches were said to carry blackthorn walking sticks to cause local mischief. Witches and heretics were burned on blackthorn pyres. In medieval times, the Devil was said to prick his follower's fingers with the thorn of a blackthorn tree. Blackthorn can be used in spells of protection as well. In Irish tales, when running from giants, heroes were helped when they threw a twig of blackthorn behind them as it would take root and form an impenetrable barrier.

In England, witches would carve the Norse rune thorn on a blackthorn stave for protection. In Sleeping Beauty, blackthorn forms the thick, impenetrable thorn bramble that hides the magic castle from all intruders, including princes, who in order to prove worthy, must cut their way through this barrier to rescue the princess.

Blackthorn is said to bloom on Christmas Eve, as is the holy thorn at Glastonbury. It is one of the trees, which were reputed to form the thorny crown of Christ at His crucifixion. If blackthorn grows near its sister plant, hawthorn, the site is said to be especially magical. Blackthorn often topped the Maypole entwined with hawthorn and is called 'Mother of the Woods.'

At New Year, farmers made blackthorn crowns, and then burned them in the New Year's fire. The ashes were then used to fertilize the fields. Blackthorn was sometimes woven into wreaths with mistletoe to bring luck in the coming year, and the garlands used to wassail the Apple trees.

The Irish cudgel is called a bata, or more popularly, a shillelagh, *named for the Shillelagh forest near Arklow, in County Wicklow.* Young lads were trained to defend themselves with this fighting stick which was usually made from blackthorn. The black bark is renowned for being especially tough. The wood was cured by burying it in a dung heap or smearing it with butter, then placing it in the chimney.

Elder Ruis (Rue)

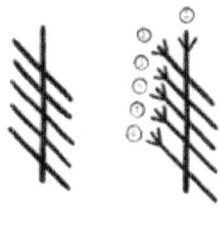

Ruis corresponds to the letter R in the Ogam alphabet and is associated with the Elder tree. This symbol represents transition, maturity and change.

Ruis pronounced: roosh

Status: Shrub

Element: Water

Gender: Feminine

Celtic Thirteenth Month: Last 3 days of October

Powers: Elder brings the eternal turning of life and death, birth and rebirth.

Keywords

Tree of the Cailleach, cycles, endings, beginnings, life/death, change, breakdown, transition. 3-fold aspects of time, existence and Goddess, regret, karma.

Deities associated with Elder

Holda, Venus, the old crone aspect of the triple Goddess, Freya, Aphrodite, Hel, Hela, Hilde, The White Lady.

Tree Description

Elder is found throughout Europe apart from the far north and can reach up to 10m high. Its bark is brown and deeply furrowed, although on younger branches it is smooth. Inside its twig the wood is soft and pithy. The leaves are arranged oppositely and are pinnate with 2-3 leaflets. Each leaf may vary from rounded to narrow oval, can be 5–30 cm long, and have serrated margins. They bear large clusters of small white or cream-coloured flowers in late spring. These smell of cats and are about 10-20cm across. They stand erect but bend under the weight of the small black, blue-black, or red berries.

Uses

Elderberry fruit or flowers are used as dietary supplements for minor diseases such as flu, colds, constipation, and other conditions, often served as a tea, extract, or in a capsule.

Whilst there is insufficient research to know its effectiveness for such uses, no illnesses caused by elderflower have been reported. Many species are widely cultivated for their ornamental leaves, flowers and fruit. Its hollow branches have proved useful for all manner of pipes and bellows; in fact, its name probably originates with the Anglo-Saxon *eller*, meaning a kindler of fire.

Interesting Spiritual Information

Elder is sacred to the White Lady. The Druids would use this tree to both bless and curse. If you stand underneath the elder in at Midsummer, it might help you to see the Fey. Elder wands are also used to drive out evil spirits or thought forms. Linked to the eternal turnings of life and death, birth and rebirth. It represents the end in beginning and the beginning in the end, life in death and death in life. The casting out of the old year and the renewal and creativity of the new. The timelessness of the cycle by which the fading of old age is always balanced by the new start of birth.

Elder can regrow any damaged branches with ease, rooting quickly from any part. In Norse mythology, Freya used the black elder as her home. In medieval times it was the house of witches and was thought to be unlucky or dangerous if you slept beneath its branches or tried to cut it down.

Tree Medicine

Black elder leaves can be used as an insecticide in the garden or as a repellent. Its berries are mildly laxative. Tea for purifying the blood can be made from the flowers and wine from its fruit. Fresh leaves can be used in compresses applied to surface wounds.

Elder flower water is still used in pharmacy as a vehicle for eye and skin lotions (see below). Elderflower can be used for swollen sinuses (sinusitis), colds, influenza (flu), swine flu, bronchitis, diabetes, and constipation. It is also used to increase urine production (as a diuretic), to increase sweating (as a diaphoretic), and to stop bleeding.

Elder is used in herbal medicine with the flowers and berries being the safest parts of the tree. The bark can be very purgative and the leaves toxic in the wrong dosage. Elders can be used as a flu remedy and to boost the immune system.

Elderflowers can be made into teas, infusions, tinctures and syrups for internal use. As a tea use for cleansing the kidneys, blood and the skin, as it opens up the pores. For colds or fever, drink plenty of hot elderflower infusion to induce sweating. It acts as a mucous membrane tonic to clear up catarrh, sinusitis and hay fever.

It is used as a cold infusion to bathe sore inflamed eyes, and to alleviate hot itchy skin (measles, chickenpox, eczema, dermatitis etc.) A salve made from elderflowers, olive oil and beeswax is known to be an old remedy for burns, chapped hands, chilblains, cuts and sores.

Elderberries, full of vitamin C are good for flu, coughs and colds. They are also tonic to the blood and helpful for gout, rheumatism and nerve pains.

In 1990, Bulgarian scientists found that Elderflowers had an antiviral action against herpes simplex type 1 (virus which causes cold sores).

Herbal Medicine: Sambucus nigra

Common Name: Elder, black elder, European elder.

Parts Used: Leaf, flower and berry.

Overview: The berries are used medicinally for colds, coughs, colic, sore throats, asthma and influenza. The leaves in salves are good for skin conditions.

The flowers are infused for fevers, measles, severe bronchial and lung problems.

For flu, the remedy is a mixture of elderflower, yarrow and peppermint teas. 2 teaspoons of the herb per cup of water, steep for 20 mins and take up to 3 cups per day. Elderflower cordial is another healthy benefit of this tree.

Internally:

Flowers

Arthritis – Anti-flammatory, stimulates sweating and the passing of urine which assists in removing inflammatory waste products from around joints.

Catarrh: By improving the functioning of mucous membranes lining the ears, nose and throat they help clear catarrh in these areas.

Colds, influenza and other infections of the respiratory tract: Enhance the non-specific immune response, gently stimulate sweating in a fever, regulate temperature control and so help pass infections off faster with less severe symptoms.

Hay fever: Combination of antiallergic, anti-inflammatory and mucous membrane soothing properties provide an excellent hay fever remedy.

Sinusitis, ear infections: Anti-inflammatory, immunostimulating and mucous membrane toning effects, antiallergic for year-round sinusitis (perennial rhinitis).

Berries

Cancer prevention: Anthocyanins have potent antioxidant effects.

Viral infections: Colds, influenza, viral infections of the upper respiratory tract.

Convalescence, debility, fatigue: The nutritional content can assist recovery and help improve energy levels.

Leaves

Bruises, sprains and chilblains and wounds.

Preparations

Flowers

Tea: For best effects drink as hot as possible, for colds and influenza drink frequently (up to 6 cups a day), otherwise drink 2-4 cups a day. For a diuretic effect, the cold tea is thought to be more effective than the hot.

Tincture: 1-5ml, three times a day, in warm water, between meals.

Cream: Apply over maxillary sinus area (on the cheeks either side of the nose).

Foot bath: For night-time coughs and fevers in children, use a foot bath before going to bed.

Eyewash: For conjunctivitis. Apply twice a day (morning and evening) or as frequently as required.

Eye compress: For tired or inflamed eyes. Apply lukewarm tea on cotton wool pads to the lids of the closed eyes for 5-10 minutes as required.

Compress: For chilblains. Apply to the chilblains for 5-10 minutes, 3-5 times a day.

Gargle: For sore throats. Gargle for several minutes frequently until the soreness resolves.

Flower water: Use neat for compresses, it has a cooling and soothing effect on the skin.

Berries:

Juice: 10mls, twice a day, in warm water, between meals.

Food: Cook and sweeten with brown sugar (elderberry rob) to make a nutritious and immune stimulating jam.

Cautions: The flowers and berries are considered to be very gentle, safe and well tolerated.

Ogam Channel Healing Guide

Spiritual/Mind: Beginnings Bereavement issues Breakdowns Changing cycles Dealing with changes Dealing with death Dealing with karma Deflated Depression Dramas of living life Endings Exhaustion Finding love within Life issues Living with the Goddess Regrets Renewing life energies Terminal illness Transitions Trauma of injury

Head/Neck: Cold Sores Ear Infections Epilepsy Eye and skin complaints Nerve pains Sinusitis Sore throats Toothache

Chest: Asthma Catarrh Colic Coughs/ colds Diabetes Flu -symptoms Hay-fever Influenza Purifying the blood Severe- bronchial and lung problems

Stomach: Constipation

Kidneys: Diuretic Kidney

Skin: Bruises Chapped hands Chicken pox Chilblains Dermatitis Eczema Measles Skin conditions Surface wounds Warts

Skin: Burns

Muscles: Sprains

Joints: Arthritis Rheumatism

Cancer: Cancer prevention

General: Fatigue

Flower Remedy

Elder flower remedy helps when you are feeling tired all the time, lacking vital energy and in danger of becoming depressed. It stimulates the renewal of your life energies and helps rejuvenate your physical and spiritual self. How you show yourself to the world is a direct reflection of how you actually see yourself. Remember that energy follows thought. So be the beautiful person that you actually are and renew yourself in the knowledge that you are perfect in every way.

Notes

The elder has strong associations with femininity and the Goddess and is often called 'Our Lady.' It can symbolise the 3 aspects of the triple Goddess: maiden, mother and hag. The elder was said to be one of the trees favoured by the Sidthe (fairies).

Folklore

In some parts of Scotland, it was seen very much like the rowan for its ability to ward off evil spells and witchcraft. Crosses made of elder twigs hung over stables and barns to protect livestock. Drivers of hearses carried whip-handles made of elder to ward off evil influences.

In Ireland, elder was a sacred tree, and it was forbidden to break even one twig.

If an elder tree was cut down, a spirit known as the *elder mother* would be released and take her revenge. The tree could only safely be cut while chanting a rhyme to her, 'Old Woman, give me some of thy wood and I will give thee some of mine when I grow into a tree.' If this course of action did not take place, ill-luck would befall the lumberjack.

In Denmark, peasants would never cut down an elder for fear of Hyldemor, the elder mother, who dwelt in its trunk. In Christian times, the elder mother, who had once been a powerful female figure venerated for the healing properties of her tree, became feared as a witch.

In Ireland, witches were thought to use elder boughs as magic horses, while in England the crooked-branched tree was thought to be the form of a bent old witch, who would bleed if she were cut. According to some legends, witches would often turn themselves into elder trees, one witch, was known to have turned an invading Danish king and his men into stone, thus creating the Rollright Stones in Oxfordshire. These stones are associated with powerful healing and divination qualities.

The tree became synonymous with the Devil, as many people feared burning elder logs in case, they brought the Devil himself into the house. In other parts of the British Isles the elder retained many of its magical associations. Should you wash your eyes in the green juice of the wood, you might well see fairies and witches.

If you stood under an elder at Samhain in Scotland, you would see the faery host riding by. Elderberries plucked on Midsummer's Eve were said to grant magical powers.

In the Isle of Man, elders are known as the main dwelling-place for elves, and that an elder tree planted outside the cottage door kept witches away. In other places too it was viewed favorably as a benevolent, protective tree. Much like the willow, it seems to have strong feminine associations.

The herbalist John Evelyn declared: *If the medicinal properties of the leaves, bark, berries, etc. were thoroughly known, I cannot tell what our countryman could ail for which he might not fetch a remedy from every (elder) hedge either for sickness or wound.*

13

Pine   Ailim   (Elation)

Ailim corresponds to the letter A in the Ogam alphabet and is associated with the Pine/Fir tree. This symbol represents clarity of vision, awareness and understanding.

Ailim pronounced: AE-luhm

Status: Shrub

Element: Air, Fire

Gender: Masculine

Powers: Ailim brings high views and long sight which give warning and clarity.

Keywords

Elation, ecstasy, enthusiasm, awe, high views and long sight, perspective, understanding, great realizations, emotional expression.

Deities associated with Pine
Osiris, Cybele, Dionysus/Bacchus, Erigone, Icarius, Pitthea, Pittheus.

Tree Description

There is only one native British pine, *Pinus sylvestris,* which can also be found in the southern mountains throughout Europe. It grows to 35-40m and is wild in Scotland in open forests with rich ground flora but is widely naturalized on heaths in England and Wales. In Scotland the shape of the tree starts as a conical tree but develops into a more flat-topped shape later in life. The other races always remain conical.

The bark is brown at the base and develops deep crocodile-like fissures. On the upper part of the tree the colour changes from rusty brown to orange-red and cracked into smaller smooth plates. Its leaves are fat, blue-grey needles in pairs on tiny wooden short shoots, as dense tufts near the end of the twigs and have a brown sheathed base. The male flowers arrive as a yellow cluster around the base of the young shoots in May but fall quickly. The female cones start as green, but mature in three years to become a grey, oval cone about 4-7 cm long.

Uses

Used in building as house joists, rafters and floors, telegraph poles and furniture. They were also used in ship building as the sap yielded a high content of resin which also meant that the wood was slow to decay. Its straight, flexible tall trunks were ideal for masts, spars and planking which was sealed with pitch made from the resin (also sealed casks like beer casks). Its wood wool was used in stuffing cushions and also as packing material. It is used as an essential oil. Vegetable tar from its roots is used to stimulate hair growth.

Interesting Spiritual Information

Pine gives us high views and long sight, seeing ahead over long distances, giving a clear view of what is beyond and yet to come, learning from past mistakes, to take care in choices. Objectivity, perspective, secrets, foresights. A dawning of understanding of something that we are part of.

If guilt is felt, use it to clear the slate with those you have hurt and renew your relationship. As the guilt is released, you will find that creativity comes forward in abundance. It has a very powerful and refreshing energy and is fast effective. Pine radiates Chi, nourishes the blood, strengthens the nervous system and helps contribute to long lives. They help nurture souls and spirits.

Tree Medicine

Its needles give a source of vitamin C and can help to loosen a tight chest. Kernels used as a restorative (beaten into emulsion with barley water) after a long illness. The resin and needles of the pine have been used, particularly as an inhalant, to treat respiratory problems, and also have antiseptic and disinfectant qualities. Pine needle tea: antiseptic, astringent, inflammatory, antioxidant, expectorant, high in Vitamin C for colds – flu – coughs, congestion, and even scurvy. Shikimic acid, the main ingredient in Tamiflu, is harvested from pine needles in Asia. Pine bark contains pycnogenol which is high in antioxidant flavonoids which combine to aid circulation and strengthen capillaries encouraging blood flow to the extremities of the body.

It can prevent damage to blood vessels and decrease blood clotting which may help prevent deep vein thrombosis during long flights. Good for reducing swelling and bruises. It may also be good for the common circulatory disorder, Reynauds disease. A French double-blind trial using 300mg per day, resulted in therapeutic effects in just 4 weeks. It is also said that Fir energy is good for broken bones.

Herbal Medicine: Pinus SPP.

Common Names: Pine/fir.

Parts Used: Needle, twig and knot of the wood.

Overview: The needles and young twigs of the white pine (Pinus strobus, Pinus alba) can be made into infusions for coughs and as an anti-scorbutic; It is high in vitamin C; use 2 teaspoons per cup of water and simmer for 20 mins.

The knot of the wood is boiled with angelica, acanthopanax, quince and mulberry branches to make a bath for arthritis and rheumatism.

Pine needles can be simmered into massage oils. The oil can also be used externally to relieve rheumatic pain, chronic bronchitis, sciatica, pneumonia and nephritis. Cover needles with a good quality olive oil and simmer at a low heat for 20 min. The resin will heal kidneys, liver and lungs. The scent is also calming to both lungs and your nerves.

Cautions: None found.

Ogam Channel Healing Guide

Spiritual/Mind: Balance   Brings you great realizations   Calmness   Centred   Creativity   Divine–harmony   Elation   Ecstasy   Emotional Expression   Enthusiasm   Fears   Feelings-of guilt   Forward planning   Looking and planning ahead   Nurturing spirituality   Giving you good perception of events/ people/ situations   Great realizations   High views   Peaceful   Persistence   Restorative after a long illness   Understanding   Weathering the storm

Head: Nervous system   Sciatica

Chest: Blood clotting   Colds   Congestion   Common circulatory disorders   Coughs   Chronic bronchitis   Excellent for getting fast energy and conserving it   Flu   Respiratory problems   Pneumonia

Lymph Glands: Increasing body immunity

Urinary: Kidney stones   Nephritis

Skin: Eczema

Muscles: Inflammations, bruises, swellings Relieves the muscles

Bones: Broken bones

Joints: Rheumatism   Arthritis   Other joint diseases

General: Antiseptic and disinfectant Detoxifying Disinfectant qualities   Scurvy

Flower Remedy

Pine helps us when we self-blame ourselves unjustly for things that have been done or undone. When we feel guilty of events outside of our control but have assumed responsibility for other's mistakes. Because of this we end up suffering needlessly and can end up saying *sorry* all the time.

To take action against this feeling, we have to acknowledge our own faults without dwelling on them, and when we can, put right what we have done wrong. But it is also important to realise when we are blameless, when we have done our best, and when we are content.

Notes

Pine's old name is, 'the sweetest of woods.' Fir is a tree of the three Brighids, representing the transformation of weakness to strength; beginning of the path to finding truth and life; a great transformation coming.

Folklore

In ancient Greece, the pine was sacred to Dionysus/Bacchus mythology surrounding the vine and wine making, most probably as a fertility symbol. The Corinthians were ordered by the Delphic Oracle to worship the pine along with Dionysus as a god. As a symbol of royalty, the pine was also associated with the Greek goddess Pitthea.

The pine was the sacred tree of the Mithraic cult in ancient Rome. During the Roman holiday of Saturnalia (Dec. 17-25th), they would decorate pine trees with ornaments (made in the image of Bacchus) such as *oscilla*, and little clay dolls known as *sigillaria*. For the Romans the pine was worshiped during the spring equinox festival of Cybele and Attis. Because it was an evergreen tree the pine would have symbolised immortality.

Pagan Europe lit heaped bonfires of pine branches at the Winter Solstice. It was designed as a magical act to bring the sun back from the depths of winter underworld.

Pine trees were a great symbol of the Germanic mid-winter festival of Yule, where yule logs and trees were decorated with many shiny objects. It was this custom that was the start of decorating the modern Christmas tree.

Many traditional fairy tales, ghost stories and mysterious events grew out of the dark and foreboding coniferous trees of the Black Forest in Germany.

Along Norway's coast there is a large rain forest of pine, spruce and other trees that provide a unique ecosystem for Scandinavia.

In the dry grasslands of eastern Siberia, there are many Scots pine groves or shamanic forests, considered sacred by the Buriats (a Mongolian people), who lived around the southern end of Lake Baikal. In respect for the gods and spirits of the wood, these groves had to be approached and entered in silence.

In Scotland, there used to be a superstition about cutting down pine trees for use in shipbuilding during the waning of the moon, as the tidal influence of the moon apparently affected the resin content of the wood. Today, botanists recognise the complexities of sap flow in plants which are affected by the gravitational cycles of the moon.

It used to be said that the Scots pine acted as a marker in the landscape for burial places of warriors, heroes and chieftains.

Further south where it might have been more unusual to see a Scots pine, they can be seen to mark ancient cairns, trackways and crossroads. In England they were also used on the edges of meadows where passing drovers and their herds could spend the night.

Furze, Gorse   Ohn   (Collecting)

Furze or gorse corresponds to the letter O (ohn, onn) in the Ogam alphabet and is associated with the Furze or gorse bush. This symbol represents determination, collecting and passion.

Ohn pronounced: Uhn

Status: Chieftain-tree

Element: Fire

Gender: Masculine

Powers: Ohn is good at collecting.

Keywords

Collecting, in-gathering, sweetness, valuable things, a magpie, skill at collecting, life changing information, sexuality, passion.

Deities associated with Furze

Jupiter, Thor, Lugh.

Tree Description

Furze or gorse is native to parts of Western Europe and northwest Africa. Furze forms a heavily branched, stunted shrub usually about six feet high. It is found in rough pastures, heaths and rocky places, preferring a dry soil. The word furze is derived from the Anglo-Saxon name *fyrs*, and gorse from the Anglo Saxon *gorst*, which means *a waste*, this refers to the open moorlands where it is often found. As it is dense and has thorns, making it an excellent hedging plant, it can be also be used as a barrier to protect young tree seedlings in coppices and as cover for game birds.

Gorse has green stems, with very small leaves and is adapted to dry growing conditions. The shoots have modified into branched thorns 1–4 cm long, which almost completely replaces the leaves as the plant's functioning photosynthetic organs. The leaves of young plants are trifoliate, and as they mature, reduce to scales or small spines. All the species have yellow flowers, with some having a very long flowering season.

Uses

Chopped up branches were placed in vegetable beds to keep mice and birds off the crops.

Furze was traditionally gathered into faggots to use as tinder to start fires. In 1864 it was cultivated in Surrey and other English counties especially for this purpose, being popular with bakers who used it as fuel for their ovens.

Due to the high concentration of oil in its leaves and branches, it catches fire easily and burns well, giving off a heat almost equal to that of charcoal. Because older plants can carry a lot of dead wood, furze can be a hazard in hot, dry summers. The ashes have a high alkali content and can be mixed with animal fat to produce clay, or to form a soap substitute. The ashes were also spread onto the fields to improve the soil.

Furze (specifically the fresh spouts of furze and grass) was used as fodder for animals, with an acre of it providing enough winter feed for up to six horses. It actually contains half the protein content of oats. The branches were run through stone mills or hit with wooden mallets to crush the thorns and bring the wood to a moss like consistency, making it more palatable for the cows and sheep. Bushes were often deliberately burnt down to encourage new growth.

In Eire the flowers were used to flavour and add colour to whiskey and the Danes were reputed to use them to make beer. They have also been used to make wine and tea. Flower buds mixed with a blade of mace and some peppercorns, in a white wine vinegar and salt solution, makes a fine pickle. Gorse flowers are edible and can be used in salads, tea and to make a non-grape-based fruit wine. Gorse wood has been used to make small objects; being non-toxic, it is especially suited for cutlery. As the wood is unstable and prone to warping it is not used for construction. The bark and its flowers produce a fine yellow dye.

Interesting Spiritual Information

Both wood and the blossoms are burnt for protection and preparation for conflict. A gathering together of sweetness and value, or a skill at collecting. It means either that circumstances around you on your path through life are gathering together towards a goal or destination you require, or that you will be enabled to collect together for yourself the elements you seek in order to attain such an end. Due to the thorny nature of the plant, it is often viewed as having protective powers.

Tree Medicine

Culpepper states in his herbal, that furze was good to open obstructions of the liver and spleen: *A decoction made with the flowers therof hath been found effectual against the jaundice and also to provoke urine, cleanse the kidneys from gravel or stone ingendered in them.*

Studies in the nineteenth century confirmed that the high alkaline content of the plant had a purgative effect. An infusion of the blooms, as a drink, was given to children suffering from scarlet fever. It was also used to cleanse the home: ... *against fleas, take this same wort, with its seed sodden; sprinkle it into the house; it killeth the fleas.*

Its flowers have been used in the treatment of jaundice, scarlet fever, diarrhoea and kidney stones.

Ogam Channel Healing Guide

Spiritual/Mind: Cleansing Collecting Emotional Security Frustration Gathering Hopelessness Jealousy Joy Life-changing information Mental-pressures Protection Restlessness Restoring Hope Passion Sexuality Sweetness Uncertainty

Head/neck: Jaundice Scarlet fever

Stomach: Diarrhoea

Liver: Liver

Urinary: Kidney stones Spleen

General: Fleas

Flower Remedy

Gorse is the remedy for people who have given up belief and hope. Gorse people willfully refuse to be encouraged, as they believe that their case is hopeless. If ill, they may think themselves incurable, and that nothing can be done.

Gorse is a remedy for *uncertainty*, as the main problem with Gorse people is their loss of faith. If persuaded to see things in a different light, there is usually a way forward. It helps ease frustration, restlessness, and jealousy, and helps promote emotional security and a feeling of deep inner joy.

Notes

Gorse represents a coming together of circumstances for you on your life journey destination, or the fact that you will be able to collect together all that you need at this time to be able to attain the end you wish.

Folklore

Furze is closely associated with the sun god Lugh, the Celtic god of light and also with the Spring Equinox, as it is one of the only plants at that time to be in full flower. It is also attached to festivals during spring and summer months as a symbol of the power of the sun. In Brittany, on August 1st, the Celtic festival of Lugnasdagh, is known as, The Festival of Golden Gorse. As an evergreen which flowers the whole year round, it is seen to carry within it a spark of the sun's life-giving energy, through the dark winter months. It is a symbol of encouragement and a promise of good things to come. Furze tells us to remain focused and optimistic, even in those periods of difficulty which we all experience.

It provides a large supply of pollen for the bees coming out of hibernation. Honey, known as the Celtic symbol of wisdom, is the product of the bee's hard work and dedication. It is a metaphor telling us that if we apply ourselves and keep faith in the future, we will be rewarded. No matter how bad things seem to be, there is always the possibility of periods of fertility, creativity and well-being; its thorns reminding us that there is protection from unwanted ideas or influences. As a sacred tree, furze was always included in the Celtic Beltane bonfires. The stock would be herded between these fires to receive purification and protection before being released out for summer grazing. Once this tradition ended, it stayed in another way, torches of furze were lit and carried around farm buildings and the herd to cleanse the air and protect them against sterility.

There are three species of furze, which all flower in slightly different seasons, which gives the impression that the bush is almost always in bloom. This gave the country saying, 'When the gorse is out of blossom, kissing is out of fashion.' A sprig of furze added to a bridal bouquet is a nod to the all-year-round blossom being a symbol of continuous fertility.

In Ulster, people dyed their eggs yellow by boiling them in water with furze blossom. These eggs were then used in Easter games and afterwards, those that survived were eaten. The blossom was also used to dye clothes yellow and its young shoots made a green dye. In Ireland, it is said that if you wear a piece of gorse/furze in your lapel you will never stumble. Due to its positive attributes, it is also said that furze on waste ground will raise its value. In Irish law furze was considered one of the *Losa fédo* or bushes of the wood.

Heather   Ur   (Lovers)

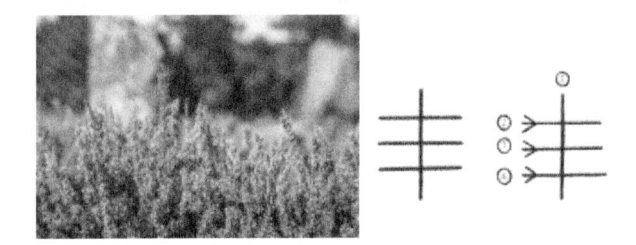

Ur corresponds to the letter U (ur, ura) in the Ogam alphabet and is associated with Heather. This symbol represents generosity, healing and success.

Ur pronounced: Oor

Status: Chieftain-tree

Element: Earth

Powers: Heather is the symbolic gateway linking the fertile earth with the inner spirit world and healing.

Keywords

Links, inner self, all-heal, development, spirit world, passion, success, dreams, small is beautiful – no need for extravagance, lovers, courtship, consummation.

Deities associated with Heather

Isis, Cybele, Erycina, Venus, Uroica.

Tree Description

Heather is a low-growing perennial shrub usually growing to 20 to 50 cm tall, or more rarely to 1m and taller. It can be found widely in Europe and Asia Minor on acidic soils in open sunny spaces as well as in moderate shade. In Europe it is the dominant plant in most heathland, moorland, some bog vegetation and acidic pine and oak woodland. It is tolerant of sheep or cattle grazing and regenerates following the occasional burning and is often managed in nature reserves.

The flowers appear late in summer; normally mauve in wild plants, but white-flowered plants can also occur. The fruit is a capsule shape.

Uses

Heather becomes an important food source for the sheep and deer which graze the tips of the plants, in winter snows. Grouse feed on the young shoots and seeds of this plant. Thomas Pennant wrote in *A Tour in Scotland* (1769) that on the Scottish island of Islay, *ale is frequently made of the young tops of heath, mixing two thirds of that plant with one of malt, sometimes adding hops.* The use of heather in the brewing of modern heather beer is carefully regulated. In Ireland the flowers were used to flavour and add colour to whiskey and the Danes were reputed to use them to make beer. With malt, heather was an ingredient in Gruit, a mixture of flavourings used in the brewing of heather-beer during the Middle Ages before the use of hops.

Heather honey is a highly valued in moorland and heathland areas, with many beehives being moved there in late summer. Not always as valued as it is today, it was dismissed as *mel improbum* by Dioscurides. Heather honey has a characteristic strong taste, and an unusual texture, for being thixotropic, it exists as a jelly until stirred, when it becomes a syrup like other honey, but then sets again to a jelly. This makes the extraction of the honey from the comb difficult, and so is often sold as comb honey. Flower buds collected and potted with a blade of mace, peppercorns, mixed in a white wine vinegar and salt solution, make a nice pickle. They can also be used to make wine and tea.

White heather is regarded as being lucky in Scotland, a tradition brought from Balmoral to England by Queen Victoria and sprigs of it are often sold as a charm and worked into bridal bouquets. Heather stalks are used by a small industry in Scotland as a raw material for sentimental jewelry. The stalks are stripped of its bark, dyed in bright colours and then compressed with resin.

Heather was used for thatching. A yellow dye was derived from it and was used to tan leather. It was also twisted into strong ropes which withstood the effects of seawater. It was gathered in bundles to make a variety of besoms and brooms – heather's Latin name *Calluna* is derived from the Greek *kalluna*, meaning *to brush*. On the Isle of Lewis, they used a particular kind of hoe which had two rows of wooden teeth followed by a row of heather to help smooth the soil. Stalks of this plant were used to create musical instruments.

The calming aroma of the dried flowers helped when mattresses were stuffed with it. Long lengths of dried, flowering heather were also packed together in the bed frame, flowers at the top and leaning towards the bed head.

Interesting Spiritual Information

It has a dual aspect with mistletoe and is considered lucky, white heather is the luckiest.

Its relationship with bees has to do with the association with the spirit world: the bee travels from the heather to its hive in relation to the position and angle of the sun, it was regarded as a messenger from and to the spirit world by the Celts. It is associated with passionate love and the keeping of secrets.

Tree Medicine

Flowering shoots are used for insomnia, stomach pains, coughs, skin problems. In the Highlands the medicinal properties of an infusion of heather tops were used to treat coughs, consumption and for soothing the nerves.

Fresh or dry heather strengthens the heart and slightly raises the blood pressure. It is slightly diuretic. Heather tea is a good general tonic. It can be used as a balm to ease arthritis and rheumatism.

It has been used in traditional Austrian medicine internally as tea for treatment of disorders of the kidneys and urinary tract.

Heather tea and ointments were used to treat arthritis and rheumatism. Moorland tea made from heather flowers, was reputed to be a favourite of Robert Burns.

Culpepper states in his herbal, that furze was good to open obstructions of the liver and spleen. *A decoction made with the flowers therof hath been found effectual against the jaundice and also to provoke urine, cleanse the kidneys from gravel or stone ingendered in them.*

Studies in the nineteenth century confirmed that the high alkaline content of the plant had a purgative effect. An infusion of the blooms, as a drink, was given to children suffering from scarlet fever. It was also used to cleanse the home: ... *against fleas, take this same wort, with its seed sodden; sprinkle it into the house; it killeth the fleas.*

In homeopathy furze is used to help people who have given up hope, who have no faith in the future. It helps people to get in touch with their own inner resources and move forward by releasing courage and determination.

Heather is useful for ailments of the genitourinary systems, including stones, kidney and bladder infections, vaginal discharge, enlarged prostate, and menstrual and menopausal symptoms. It stimulates the flow of bile and urine, making it useful in cleansing and purifying teas. It is also a soothing herb and is good for spasmodic complaints in any system, including stomach and intestinal cramping and spasmodic coughs. Its soothing nature also makes it good for nervousness and insomnia. It can also be added to salves for gout and rheumatism and for soothing skin preparations. It has anti-microbial properties. Can be used as an antiseptic as it has an anti-inflammatory – astringent or clearing quality to it. It works as anti-rheumatic. Diuretic – used to treat cystitis. Also grows wild in Mexico and is used to treat cancer – the Spanish name is Cancerina or Chanclana or Alcancer

Warning: Heather may raise blood pressure slightly and should not be used by people with blood pressure issues.

Herbal Medicine: Calluna Vulgaris

Parts Used: Flowering shoot.

Overview: You can use the flowering shoots of heather for insomnia, stomach pains, coughs and skin issues. Heather is also good for working with the heart, strengthening it but be aware that it also can raise the blood pressure. It is also slightly diuretic.

It can be used fresh or dry and is simmered, 4 teaspoons to the cup, drink one half cup per day.

Cautions: None found.

Ogam Channel Physical Healing Guide

Spiritual/Mind: Confidence to court others   Courage   Courting   Consumption   Determination   Dreams   Fear   Generosity   Hopelessness   Healthy mind, body + soul   In need of courage and determination   Links to spirit world   Lifting the spirit   Good for lovers/loving   Opening up to consummation   Passion   Success   Opening -up your ability to love others   Opening your passion for things

Head/Neck: Insomnia   Nervousness

Chest: Consumption   Coughs including spasmodic cough   Raising blood pressure (Be careful)   Strengthens heart

Stomach: Intestinal cramps Spasmodic cramps   Stomach pains

Urinary: Bladder infections   Kidney and bladder infections   Kidney stones   Stimulates flow of bile and urine   Urinary tract

Female Cycles: Cystitis   Menopause   Menstrual   Vaginal discharge

Skin: Skin problems

Joints: Rheumatism   Arthritis

Glands: Enlarged Prostrate

Cancer: Cancer

General: Anti-inflammatory   Gout

Flower Remedy

Heather is for people obsessed about themselves but do not like being alone. They can latch onto you and spend all their time talking about themselves and their issues, a bit like an energy vampire. They do this until people actively avoid them which brings the loneliness people fear, because of their behaviour.

The heather remedy helps them see their own concerns in the context of other people's. They can become very good listeners and people start seeking them out for their compassion.

Notes

Heather has a dual aspect with mistletoe in the Ogam, Celtic Tree Oracle of Liz and Colin Murray. Very much considered lucky and white heather is seen as the luckiest. The bee uses the position and angle of the sun to travel back to its hive from the heather and was regarded as a messenger from and to Spirit world by the Celts. It is also associated with passionate love and keeping secrets.

Folklore

The word *Calluna* is derived from the Greek meaning *to sweep*. Heather along with the thistle, is Scotland's national flower. Scottish farmers carried torches of burning heather around their fields before midsummer to ensure good crops and around their cattle to ensure their fertility.

Heather can be used in spells relating to new beginnings, and self-discovery, enhancing physical beauty and bringing a peaceful resolution to any conflict. It is also used at initiations.

Keeping heather about the house will attract friendly spirits and will bring peace to the household. Carrying heather will attract positive energies, general good luck and protect against rape and other violent assaults, making it useful for traveling sachets.

Burning heather together with fern will aid in magic designed to bring rain. The two plants can also be bundled together and used to sprinkle water on the ground for the same purpose.

Heather helps in summoning spirits and attracts faeries to the garden. Heather is a good plant to use to make besoms and can be added to midsummer fires to ensure the fertility of the attendants. Heather is said to be stained with the blood of war in

Scotland, thus, white heather is the luckiest and the best for use in magic. Heather should be part of a bridal bouquet or the decorations to ensure good luck to the couple and peace and cooperation in their household.

Scottish legend also says that no white heather will ever grow where blood has been shed. One of the sweetest legends of Scottish folklore is that white heather only grows where fairies have been.

Mistletoe

Mistletoe works as the invisible fertility symbol with inner meaning attached and works as the inner aspect to the heather's outside aspect. By combining they help guide one into closer contact with spirit and the healing opportunities available.

Gender: Masculine

Planet: Sun

Element: Air

Powers: Protection, love, hunting, fertility. Health and exorcism.

Passion, generosity, changes, healing, luck, protection, spirituality.

Keywords

Passion, generosity, changes, healing, luck, protection, spirituality.

Deities associated with Mistletoe

Apollo, Freya, Frigga, Venus, Odin.

Tree Description

Mistletoe attaches itself to their host tree by a structure called the haustorium by which they can extract water and nutrients. It looks like a large ball and was originally referred to the species Viscum album and is the only species native to Britain and much of Europe.

It lives on trees like the oak, elm, fir, pine, apple, and elm. This plant has pointy bright red to yellowish to green flowers and have waxy, white or red berries which are poisonous to eat. It is more obvious in winter when the tree is bare.

Uses

Christmas decorations, an opportunity to kiss someone underneath it when hung as part of the Christmas celebrations. The mistletoe contains many healing properties, see below.

Interesting Spiritual Information

Is also known as All heal and Golden Bough. It is the most sacred tree of the Druids and rules the Winter Solstice. Beware though, as the berries are poisonous. Bunches of mistletoe have been hung as an all-purpose protective herb, which is a good enough reason for kissing under.

The berries are used in love incenses. It was on the sixth day of the new moon closest to the Winter Solstice, that the Druids harvested it within a great ceremony as an offering to the gods. It was seen as an offering of cosmic male fertility to the goddess of the land (the sacred womb of creation), the rite is a metaphor expressing the union from which nature emerges.

Mistletoe: Viscum Album

Folk names: Birdlime, golden bough, all heal, holy wood.

Parts used: Twig and leaf.

Overview: There are male and female plants, which get their water and minerals from the host tree and so produce their own carbohydrates via photosynthesis. Mistletoe is rich in phosphorus, magnesium, potassium and sulphur. Its proteins, polysaccharides and fat substances are strongly tumour-inhibiting. Tumour-inhibiting bacteria have also been found within the plant. It seems to increase killer cells, increase cell-mediated cytotoxic activities and augment levels of granular lymphocytes.

Mistletoe has been of benefit to many nervous conditions such as convulsions, delirium, hysteria, neuralgia, urinary disorders and heart conditions. Mistletoe strengthens the heart, glandular system and with inflammation of the pancreas It helps promote hormonal balance when taken daily for 6 months.

It is recommended for use after a stroke and will stop pulmonary and intestinal bleeding caused by dysentery and typhoid. It raises low blood pressure and lowers high blood pressure. It has been used to ease heavy menstrual flow, heart palpitations, hot flashes and anxiety which comes with the menopause. Its fresh juice has been said to increase fertility in barren women.

Caution: The berries should not be used for internal consumption. They can be used in salves and washes for wounds.

Ogam Channel Physical Healing Guide

Spiritual/Mind: All Heal   Changes   Exorcism   Fertility   Generosity   Healing   Love, open up to its influences   Luck   Passion   Prophetic Visions   Protection   Male fertility   Female Goddess   Spirituality

Head: Anxiety (Menopause)   Convulsions   Delirium   Hot flashes (Menopause)   Hysteria   Nervous conditions   Neuralgia

Heart: Blood pressure high and low Heart conditions Heart palpitations Strokes

Stomach: Dysentery Typhoid

Intestines: Intestinal bleeding

Urinary: Urinary disorders

Glands: Glandular system Pancreas Hormonal balance Lymphatic system

Women's cycles: Fertility as in Barren women Menopause Menstruation

Skin: Wounds

Notes

The mistletoe was not officially part of the Celtic Ogam but was a sacred plant to the Druids. Its Irish name is *drualus*, a word which is related to the word *druid*. The root of both words refers to the sacred oak tree, upon which mistletoe grows. It is also referred to as the *blank* Ogam, which in runic traditions, is called *Wyrrd*, representing the unknown or unknowable. It is associated with the element of air; its ruling planet is the sun, which is also fitting as it is the turning point of the solar year.

Folklore

In Greek mythology, mistletoe was believed to be the Golden Bough of Aeneas, who was led from Troy by Venus to found Rome. The early Greeks also thought that the oak mistletoe had mystical powers and could extinguish fire, as it can grow either as a parasite on other plants or on its own.

The Druids regarded mistletoe as the most sacred of trees because it grew between earth and sky, without touching either. Within its symbolism also included the unknown, the life force, divine semen (its white berries resembling semen, and its red berries resembling women's menstrual blood), and immortality. It was cultivated specifically on the sixth night of the moon, cut from the oak with a golden sickle and caught in a white lined cloth, for if it touched the ground it would lose its magic. This act symbolized the emasculation of the Old King by his successor. At the same time, two white bulls would be sacrificed so that the receivers of the mistletoe would prosper.

In Norse mythology, mistletoe was reportedly what killed Baldr, the god of light and beauty.

Its protective qualities led to branches being hung in the house to ward off evil spirits and witches. This developed into the custom of decorating houses with branches of mistletoe at Christmas. Christians believed that mistletoe was a tree that furnished the cross, and then because of that act, shrivelled after the crucifixion to become a parasitic vine.

It has been used in spells and rituals to produce an aphrodisiac effect, or aid in fertility and love. It has also been used as a sacred form of protection and produce prophetic visions. Herbalists in Europe have used its leaves and twigs in treating circulatory and respiratory system problems. It has also been used to treat hypertension and epilepsy, as well as menstrual problems, haemorrhage, and headache. It is said that you can blend the mistletoe's healing energy with the tree it is growing on, as in mistletoe and oak, poplar etc…

It is interesting that the berries which ripen in midwinter can be found on the same plant with its open flowers, green berries, and immature leaves at the same time. It also owns the powers of being able to grow in any direction it chooses, germinating in the light where other plants prefer the dark. Mistletoe does not follow a cycle like other plants. It is said that in this way, it simulates the timelessness of the Faerie realms, where time is immaterial.

Aspen   Eadha   (Spiritedness)

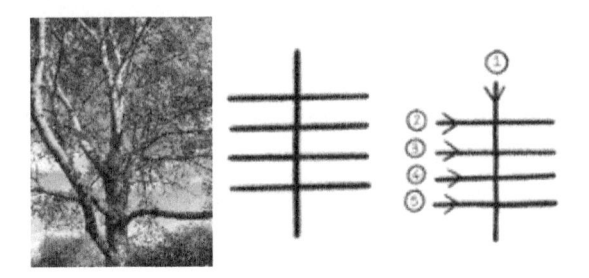

Ebha, Eadha corresponds to the letter E in the Ogam alphabet and is associated with the Aspen tree. This symbol represents endurance, courage and self-confidence.

Eadha pronounced: Ed-yuh

Status: Shrub

Element: Air

Gender: Masculine

Powers: Eadha is the messenger of the wind, creating a shield and beating adversity.

Keywords

Overcoming, willpower, sensitivity, adversity, help and rebirth, preventing illness, resistance, shield, association with speech, language and the winds, ability to endure and conquer problems, doubts, conquering fear, self-confidence.

Deities associated with Aspen

Persephone, Hades.

Tree Description

Aspen is a species of poplar native to cool temperate regions of Europe and Asia. It flourishes beside rivers, marshes and other watery areas. It is hardy and tolerates long, cold winters and short summers. Aspen is dioecious, so individual trees are either male or female (in contrast to most trees, where male and female flowers occur on the same tree).

The tree flowers in March and April, before the leaves appear, with both the male and female trees producing catkins. Pollinated female catkins ripen in early summer and release tiny fluffy seeds in summer. Its main method of reproduction is vegetative (asexual), as it spreads by its root sprouts, which may be produced up to 40m from the parent tree. A large number of new shoots may be produced like this, especially after major disturbances such as fires.

It is also known as quaking aspen; it is a beautiful tree with shimmering foliage.

Mature trees can grow up to 25m. The bark is generally smooth and silvery-green, although older trees may be covered with lichen, which gives the trunk a black appearance, and is often pitted with diamond-shaped pores, called lenticels. The uppermost branches are often bent over horizontally. Twigs are dark brown, slender and slightly glossy. Its leaves are almost round with large, irregular blunt teeth. The leaf stalks are flattened and flexible near the leaf blade, which is why they flutter so easily. Young leaves are coppery coloured before becoming green, then turn a bright yellow or occasionally red before falling in autumn. The upper leaves are green, and the underneath is silver.

Uses

Aspen wood is white and soft, but fairly strong. It is used in making matches and paper where its low flammability makes it safer to use than most other woods. Shredded aspen wood is used for packing and stuffing, sometimes called excelsior (wood wool).

Aspen flakes are the most common species of wood used to make oriented strand boards. It is also a popular animal bedding, as it lacks the phenols associated with pine and juniper, thought to cause respiratory system ailments in some animals. Heat-treated aspen is a popular material for the interiors of saunas. While standing trees sometimes tend to rot from the heart outward, the dry timber weathers extremely well, becoming silvery-grey and resistant to rotting and warping. It has traditionally been used for rural construction in the northwestern regions of Russia (roofing in the form of thin slats). Aspen wood is lightweight, and used for making oars and paddles, surgical splints and wagon bottoms. Its wood was also used in the making of shields. Quaking aspen inner bark was widely used by the Native Americans tribe of Apaches and others as a food, for themselves and their horses.

Interesting Spiritual Information

The leaves move dramatically in the wind and is commonly referred to as the talking, whispering and quivering tree. It has the power to protect you from your fears, injury and death, it can even intervene between you and your worldly problems. The aspen can help you with the power of speech and language because of its association with the wind (the messengers of the gods). Heracles wore a crown of poplar leaves when he retrieved Cerberus from Hades, and the upper surface of the leaves was turned dark by Hades smoky fumes.

Tree Medicine

Aspen bark is used for fevers, urinary tract infection and

gonorrhoea. The sticky winter buds can be used for tea and externally for cuts, wounds, salves for sore throats. A decoction of bark can be used to treat rheumatism, arthritis, prostate discomforts, back trouble (sciatica), nerve pain (neuralgia/ headaches), and bladder problems. The most important compound in aspen is salicin, a type of phenolic glycoside with anti-inflammatory and antiseptic actions.

Aspen's phenolic glycosides and tannins are responsible for the astringent properties of its bark and leaves and have been traditionally used for treating diarrhea. Aspen is a tree. The bark and leaf of the tree are used to make medicine.

Aspen is used in combination with other herbs for treating joint pain (rheumatism), prostate discomforts, back trouble (sciatica), nerve pain (neuralgia), and bladder problems.

How does it work?

Aspen contains a chemical that is very similar to aspirin. This chemical, known as salicin, may help reduce swelling (inflammation).

Overview Information: Aspen is a tree. The bark and leaf of the tree are used to make medicine.

Aspen is used in combination with other herbs for treating joint pain (rheumatism), prostate discomforts, back trouble (sciatica), nerve pain (neuralgia), and bladder problems.

How does it work?

The bark and the leaves are mildly diuretic, expectorant and stimulant. The bark is therefore anodyne, anti-inflammatory and febrifuge. It is used especially in treating rheumatism and fevers, and also to relieve the pain of menstrual cramps. Additional health benefits of aspen include the alleviating skin conditions like eczema or acne, relieving fever, helping in frostbite healing and treating urinary tract infections.

Herbal Medicine: Populus species

Common Names: See under species used.

Species used: Several populas species are used in medicine including *P. alba* (white poplar), *P. nigra* (black poplar), *P. tremula* (aspen), *P. tremuloides* (quaking aspen). Also related are *P. x candicans* (Blam of Gilead), *Salix alba, salix nigra*.

Range: Eurasia (*P. alba* and *P. nigra*), Eurasia, North Africa (*P. tremula*), North America and Canada (*P. tremuloides*).

Parts Used: Bark.

Overview: Poplar trees are grouped together as they are all used medicinally in similar ways. Related to the willow trees they contain salicylates, which are anti-inflammatory. Poplar bark is useful for treating muscle and joint aches and pains, also in colds, other febrile infections and it can ease period pains.

Phytochemicals: Phenolic glycosides (including salicin and populin), tannins.

Actions: Anti-inflammatory, anodyne, astringent.

Indications

Internally: Arthritis, fevers, period pains, rheumatism, urinary infections such as cystitis.

Preparations

Internally: The bark is given as a tincture or as a decoction.

Cautions: None found.

Ogam Channel Healing Guide

Spiritual/Mind: Ability to endure hardships   Adversity   Anxiety   Apprehension   Asking for help in things   Conquer problems, doubts and fears   Endurance   Fears of the unknown   Fear of unknown attacks   Freeing your voice   Night terrors   Preventing -illness   Rebirth   Resistance   Self-confidence   Self-love   Sensitivity   Speech and language   Strengthening Will power   Terror

Head/Neck: Epilepsy syndrome-(FIRES) Headaches Neuralgia Protection from fear, worries, paranoia   Sciatica (back pain)   Sore throats

Chest: Fevers

Stomach: Diarrhoea

Urinary: Bladder issues   Urinary tract infection

Women's cycles: Menstrual cramps Period pain

Genital: Cystitis   Gonorrhoea

Muscle: Muscle ache

Skin: Acne   Eczema   Frostbite   Externally for cuts and wounds

Joints: Rheumatism   Arthritis.

Flower Remedy

Aspen is the remedy for fear which cause cannot be named, anxiety and apprehension. From a feeling of impending doom to real physical terror. This includes nightmares or night terrors. It does not matter even if it is just a simple worry about the unknown future, aspen will work for you, clearing them away and settling you down.

Notes

There are legends about the aspen dancing in answer to the Sidhe (fairies), whose secrets are carried on the wind. Pagan Irish had a rod or 'Fe' of aspen, marked with its Ogam symbol to measure bodies and graves. The association with the Sidhe is suggestive of a mediator between worlds. For some Ogam practitioners, aspen is placed in the forfeda Ae, with the meaning of grove or meeting place (represents communication, resolution and justice).

Folklore

A crown made of aspen leaves was found in the ancient burial mounds of Mesopotamia, dating back 3,000 BC, it was said to give its wearer the power to visit and return safely from the Underworld. Aspen crowns may have been included to allow the spirits of the dead to be reborn. Aspis, the aspen's Greek name, means shield, which was one of the many traditional uses of its wood.

It is called the whispering tree because of its rustling leaves. In ancient days the wind was regarded as the messenger of the gods and because of this, the aspen was considered sacred.

In Christian lore, the quaking poplar (aspen) was used to construct Christ's cross, and the leaves quiver when they remember this fact. It's ability to resist and shield, with its association with speech, language and the winds, indicate an endurance and conquering spirit.

The church stated that the aspen trembled because its wood was used in the crucifixion. The tree is however more known for its pagan powers which allowed communication with the gods and entrance into the Fey lands. In the Scottish Highlands it was rumoured to be connected with the Fey.

Yew   Idho   (Transition)

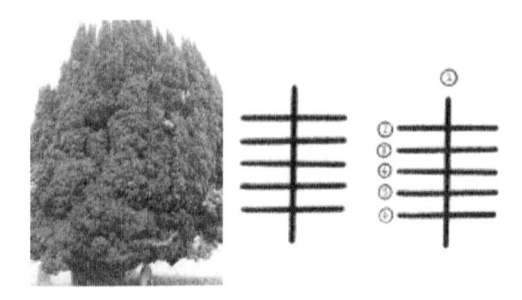

Ioho, Idho corresponds to the letter I in the Ogam alphabet and is associated with the Yew tree. This symbol represents transition, endings and change.

Idho pronounced: Ed-yoh

Status: Peasant-tree

Element: Air

Gender: Masculine

Powers: Idho represents rebirth and transformation

Keywords

Rebirth, everlasting life and death, the eternal cycle, complete change in life direction or attitude, transformation.

Deities associated with Yew

Banbha, Diane, Artemis, Persephone, Hecate, Astarte, Odin and the Crone aspect of the triple Goddess.

Tree Description

The Yew tree is a conifer native to western, central and southern Europe, northwest Africa, northern Iran and southwest Asia. It is a small to medium-sized evergreen tree, growing 10–20m tall, with a trunk up to 2m. The bark is thin, scaly reddish, which comes off in small flakes aligned with the stem.

The trunk is often fluted due to the shoots which are constantly produced from its base. The leaves are flat, dark green needles, 1–4 cm long and 2–3 mm broad, arranged spirally on the stem, but with the leaf bases twisted to align the leaves in two flat rows either side of the stem, except on its erect leading shoots where the spiral arrangement is more obvious. The leaves are poisonous as is its fruit, which is pink-red, cup shaped, looks like a berry and called an aril. The flowers which are both male and female are borne on separate trees are tiny. If knocked in the early spring, the male trees release clouds of pollen.

Uses

Wood from the yew is classified as a closed-pore softwood, similar to cedar and pine. It is easy to work with and is among the hardest of the softwoods; yet still possessing a remarkable elasticity, making it ideal for products that require springiness, such as bows.

The late Robert Lundberg, a noted luthier, performed extensive research on historical lute-making methodology, and stated in his 2002 book *Historical Lute Construction* that yew was historically a prized wood for lute construction.

Interesting Spiritual Information

Yews can often be found in churchyards, with the older ones probably pre-dating the church itself as it is very long lived (up to 2,000 years) and was an important pre-Christian tree in pagan rites. Yew is used to enhance magical and psychic abilities and induce visions. It is important to the Winter Solstice. Transformation, reincarnation, eternal life and immortality sum up its attributes. It is associated with death, rebirth, change and regeneration.

Yews place you in contact with your past. Your spiritual strength is renewed, your life is given fresh energy and you are able to understand, through the wisdom that was always there but you may have forgotten or ignored, what was, is and always will be.

Yew is another important Winter Solstice tree, working with the deities of death and rebirth. The Irish made dagger handles, bows and wine barrels. The wood or leaves were laid on graves to remind the departed spirit that death was only a short pause before rebirth.

Tree Medicine

The yew is poisonous and a violent purgative. Despite this, yew is used for treating diphtheria, tapeworms, swollen tonsils (tonsillitis), seizures (epilepsy), muscle and joint pain (rheumatism), urinary tract conditions, and liver conditions. All parts of this plant, except the fleshy fruit, are antispasmodic, cardiotonic, diaphoretic, emmenagogue, expectorant, narcotic and purgative. The leaves have been used internally in the treatment of asthma, bronchitis, hiccup, indigestion, rheumatism and epilepsy. Externally, the leaves have been used in a steam bath as a treatment for rheumatism.

A cancer drug, Taxol, has been derived from its bark and needles. Taxol has shown exciting potential as an anti-cancer drug, particularly in the treatment of breast and ovarian cancers. Taxotere has proven effective in combating lung and prostate cancer and advanced cases of breast cancer.

Herbal Medicine: Taxus baccata

Common names: Yew, English yew.

Parts Used: Needles, tips of branches, bark and leaves (needles).

Overview: This plant should not be used without professional supervision. Its main medical interest is as a source for the alkaloid taxol, used in conventional medicine to treat breast and ovarian cancer. Native American tribes used the Pacific yew for lung disorders and taxol is being also being developed as a treatment for lung cancer. The needles and branch tips have been used for lung and bladder issues, arthritis, gout and pustular skin diseases under strict professional supervision. Please note that the only safe part of the tree is aril, which is the red pithy part circling the fruit.

Cautions: The yew is poisonous,

Ogam Channel Healing Guide

Spiritual/Mind: Attitude   Change in life direction   Dealing with death   Death, dying and beyond   Expansion   Finding the peace in your heart   Higher purpose   Life purpose   Linking in with ancestors   Linking with divinity   Rebirth   Transformation (diets, life expression etc)   Unblocking life purpose

Head/Neck: Epilepsy   Tonsillitis

Chest: Asthma   Bronchitis

Stomach: Indigestion   Tapeworms

Liver: Liver

Urinary: Bladder issues   Urinary tract

Cancer: Breast cancer   Lung cancer   Ovarian cancer   Prostate cancer

Muscles: Pains

Joints: Rheumatism

Skin: Skin diseases   Pustular skin diseases

General: Diphtheria   Gout

Flower Remedies

Yew flower remedies help you to realise your life's purpose. It gets rid of that which is holding you back and pushes you into spontaneous action leading to new directions for you to grow in. Once you realise it is time for change, as in your attachment to people who are a bad influence on you, or something that is holding you back from being your true self, yew remedy will propel you forwards to help you grow, expand and find yourself rebirthing in the now. It can help you let go of whatever is blocking you achieve your higher purpose.

Notes

Yews are often found in graveyards, or old sacred places of power. They grow in a unique way, their branches grow down into the ground to form new stems which become the trunks of new trees, whilst still linked to the original tree. A new tree can also grow from the decaying mass of the old trunk. In time, they cannot be distinguished from the original tree. The yew has always been a symbol of death and rebirth, the new that springs out of the old.

Folklore

In early times, the darkly glorious yew-tree was probably the only evergreen tree in Britain. Both Druids with their belief in reincarnation, and later Christians with their teaching of the resurrection, regarded it as a natural symbol of everlasting life. The fact that it could reach a great age enriched this symbolic value.

The early Irish regarded it as one of the most ancient beings on earth. Yew is the last on a list of oldest things in a passage from the fourteenth century Book of Lismore, 'Three lifetimes of the yew for the world from its beginning to its end.'

14

Grove Koad (Communication)

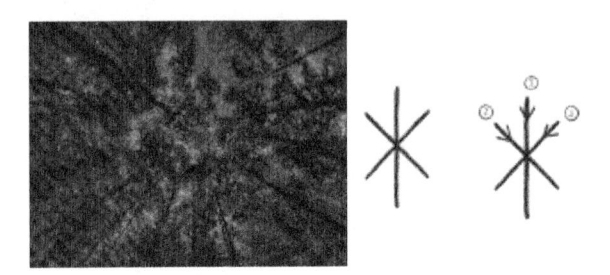

Koad corresponds to the sound Ea in the Ogam alphabet and is associated with the Druid Groves. This symbol represents communication, resolution and justice.

Koad pronounced: Kod

Element: Spirit, Earth

Powers: Koad is a sacred sanctuary of all knowledge, past, present, future.

Keywords

Revelation of all knowledge, safety, sanctuary, togetherness, unity, gathering in, collecting for use, comprehension and new deeper understanding.

Deities associated with Grove

All the deities used for Ogam work can be channelled into the grove.

Tree Description

A Koad or Grove, is a sacred circle of trees that are of special religious importance to particular cultures. It is said that the branches of these trees are never pruned or loped. Groves found in Britain are assumed to be remnants of Druidic Groves. These groves contained various types of trees, among them the oak and willow, and were found by streams. It is here all meetings by the Druids were held *in the face of the Sun and in the eye of Light*, which it is said to have given birth to the modern tradition of free speech in our democracy. It was here in the groves, that the people's grievances were heard, and judgements given that settled issues. Grove indicates all knowledge, past, present and future, where all are linked in unity, and the resolution of conflict.

Uses

Physical: By being present, you are willingly searching for a resolution of conflict and healing.

Emotional: Here you lay yourself open to the healing benefits of the Grove and its trees; the knowledge accessible to help you emotionally deal with the aspects of your life you are looking at.

Mental: Misunderstandings can be sorted if both sides meet together and work towards a common end.

Spiritual: By working with higher spiritual values, judgements made in here are seen to be above reproach. By coming together, we are a living example that can used to best teach others. Such gatherings were for both ritual purposes and for the practice of law/judgement.

Interesting Spiritual Information

In ancient times, the Druids used these Sacred Groves as places of sanctuary and worship. They were places of spiritual refuge, very much like a church, but set in the natural world. It was here that people came to calm the mind, refresh the spirit, and find comfort in times of trouble. As above so below. Wisdom unveiled, both natural and spiritual. Revolving patterns of the soul. Comprehension of all you already know or are capable of learning.

Tree Medicine

A sacred place to come and source all knowledge, all energy and divine intervention. Use meditation, healing, praying, spiritual counselling, magic and divination.

Ogam Channel Healing Guide

Spiritual/Mind: Access to allies, guides, tutors and deities Collecting information Communication Comprehension Deeper-understanding Entrance and interaction to the Akashic Records Fertility Gathering in Healing others Journey to access past, present and future knowledge Justice Liberation Light Body Meditation Personal healing Rebirth Resolution Revelation of all knowledge Safety Sanctuary Spiritual development Spiritual nourishment Togetherness Transition Transformation Union Unity

Notes

This symbol represents communication, resolution and justice. The Celts held public meetings in groves. A grove is a clearing within the forest which protected the people within from the elements. At that time, the majority of the British Isles was covered by dense forest, and so a clear space was appreciated by all and used as a sacred place. In the grove, public meetings were held to decide law and deal out punishments. A place where many people meet and carry out ceremonies and initiations would create immense energy that would be savored by all who attended them.

Folklore

In folklore across the world, trees are often said to be the homes of tree spirits. The Egyptian Book of the Dead mentions sycamores as being part of the scenery where the soul of the deceased finds blissful repose. In Greek mythology we find the female dryads, tree spirits, mainly of the oak trees. Germanic mythology as well as Celtic polytheism involved spiritual practice in sacred groves of trees.

The term, Druid, itself, derives from the Celtic word for oak. Trees are significant in many of the world's mythologies and religions and have been given deep and sacred meanings throughout the ages. They are seen as sacred symbols of growth, death and rebirth. Evergreen trees, which largely stay green throughout the yearly cycle have been considered symbols of the eternal, immortality or fertility. The Herder Symbol Dictionary says, "Psychoanalysis sees in the tree a symbolic reference to the mother, to spiritual and intellectual development, or to death and rebirth."

Across time, pilgrims have hung objects upon trees in order to establish some sort of a relationship between themselves and the tree. It could be for healing, blessings for friends and family, or just for good luck.

Trees have also associated with oracles. The oak of Dodona was tended by priests who happily lived beside it and the oaks of the Prussians were said to be inhabited by gods who would give information to those who sought it. Liz and Colin Murray introduced the Koad or Grove to this forfeda in their book of divination called Celtic Tree Oracle. In it, the grove is linked to all sacred places and is described as *all knowledge*.

In Ireland, up until the 12th century AD in Ireland, sacred trees were associated with royal sites of inauguration; it is said that the king's wand of office was broken off from these sacred trees. The ancient symbol of the Tree is seen to represent physical and spiritual nourishment, transformation and liberation, union and fertility.

A grove was as sacred as any temple, for within it was where both the physical and spiritual world met. It was used as a place of worship, for council meetings as well as for magical and healing work. Where issues were sorted out between people, or justice requested, it was in these peaceful places that people would come to meet with the Druids. Druids held such power that even the rulers would bow to their decisions in matters of state, religion and life. Both sides would state their cases and be listened to. All had the right to speak and matters were reasonably quickly settled. The Romans directive upon invading Prydain (Isle of Britain) was to break up and destroy all of the groves, such was their fear of the Druids. It is interesting to note that the grove was sacred to all Deities.

Spindle   Oire   (Revelations)

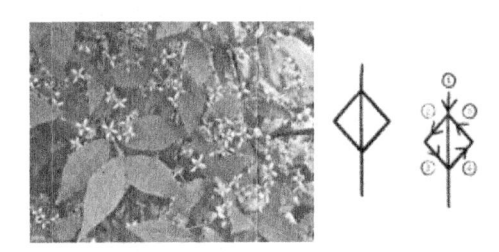

Oire corresponds to the sound oi or oe in the Ogam alphabet and is associated with the Spindle tree. This symbol represents community relationships, revelations and honour.

Oire pronounced: Ore

Element: Water

Gender: Feminine

Powers: Oire is the sweetness and revelation of Soul's desire.

Keywords

Obligations met, honour, cleansing, sweetness, delight in revelations, feminine power, seeking true self, thunder and lightning.

Deities associated with Spindle

Athena, Frigg/Freya, Minerva, The Fates.

Tree Description

The spindle grows up to about 6m tall and is most often found in scrubland, chalk and limestone ground in Britain. The tree rarely has a single trunk, though its main stems have smooth grey-green bark.

Its twigs have 4 angles, are smooth, hairless and have opposite pairs of narrow oval, pointed bright green leaves. Its flowers are small, greenish-white and appear in May. They have 4 thin, widely spaced petals, in clusters of 3-8. The fruit of the spindle tree can be found around Sept-October. The seeds are covered by the aril, which is a bright orange fleshy structure, and enclosed cherry-pink capsule.

Uses

Spindle wood was used for making spindles as in the spinning of wool. Also used in making; pegs, bobbins, skewers, knitting needles, toothpicks and shoemakers pegs as its pale-yellow wood can be easily worked. Charcoal used by artists and gunpowder can be made from the young shoots. The plant gives up oil that is used in soap making. A yellow dye can be obtained from the fleshy coating around the seeds. When alum is added, this becomes green, but both colours are short lived. The berries once baked and powdered can be used to remove lice from the hair, and it can also be used as an insecticide. Its roots are used in electrical insulation and for making plastics. The wood is extremely hard, but easily split, it is fine-grained but not durable.

Interesting Spiritual Information

The Spindle helps create firm foundations before we start to move forward to meet our appointments. To do this we need to finish what has been started to clear the decks for action. It can be used as a cleaning agent to heal emotional wounds. As its name implies, it can weave spells to bring people together and provide us with the humour needed to deal with delicate situations. We can use spindle to face our dark mirror selves and major difficulties. It is a wood that can be used as a pendulum in divination.

Tree Medicine

Spindle is a violent purgative. The root bark is alterative, cholagogue, hepatic, laxative, stimulant and tonic, although bark from the stems is sometimes employed as a substitute. In small doses it stimulates the appetite, in larger doses it irritates the intestines.

The bark is especially useful in the treatment of liver disorders which follow or accompany fevers. The seeds are strongly emetic and purgative. The fresh leaves, and the dried fruit and seeds, are used externally to treat scabies, lice (head, body or pubic), ticks and other skin parasites.

Warning: Violent purgative, all parts especially the fruit and seeds are poisonous.

Herbal Medicine: Euonymus species

Plant Family: Celastraceae.

Parts used: Bark principally but also the roots and berries.

Overview: The American and European species are used in similar ways although E. atropurpurea is used more commonly. Spindle tree bark stimulates the gall bladder and liver and has a laxative effect. The American Eclectic doctors used it for liver enlargement and as a tonic to help patients recover from malaria.

Phytochemicals: *E. atropurpurea* – cardenolide glycosides, sterols, tannins.

Actions: Anthelmintic, appetite stimulant, cholagogue, depurative, laxative.

Indications:

Internally: Constipation, skin disorders such as acne and psoriasis, worm infestation (children and adults).

Preparations

Internally: Bark as a decoction or tincture.

Cautions: The berries can cause diarrhoea and vomiting. The dosage of all parts of the spindle tree must be carefully calculated to avoid causing digestive upsets, and so it should only be taken on expert professional advice. It should not be taken during pregnancy.

Ogam Channel Healing Guide

Spiritual/Mind: Balance feelings of superiority and inferiority   Balancing your mind   Cleansing   Depression   Destiny   Energises Soul Energy   Fate   Fears   Fear of the dark   Feminine power   Honour   Meeting of obligations   Revelations   Security   Seeking true self   Self-worth   Skills   Spiritual Revelation   Survival   Sweetness   To improve relationships   Understanding your needs

Chest: Fevers   Malaria

Stomach: Appetite stimulant   Dieting   Intestinal issues   Worm infestation

Liver: Liver disorders

Organs: Gall bladder

Bowels: Constipation

Skin: Acne   Psoriasis   Scabies   Lice   Ticks   Skin parasites

Flower Remedy

Spindle flower essence helps you to understand one's true nature and your specific needs. It gives you a sense of security so that you don't feel you need to constantly compare yourself to others. It helps balance out your feelings of superiority and inferiority. It energises the soul energy in an integrated and positive way.

Notes

It is interesting to note that women were treated in a much more respected and equal way in Celtic tribes. As spinning could take a long time, one had to be quite patient whilst working. However, if the woman was highly skilled, she often made a good living which brought her high status within her clan. So, the spindle also represents skills and surviving.

Folklore

The spindle tree is used to make spindles in weaving and that is why it is called that. In Celtic tales weaving is associated with fate and destiny, as are the Norns in Nordic mythology. They are weaver goddesses who weaved the fate of the people and cut the threads which were connected to their lives when it was their time to die.

The Norse and Germanic Goddess Frigg is also associated with weaving as well as the Valkyries. Another name for the constellation of Orion was Freya's spindle. The spindle is a symbol of magic in the Norse Pagan tradition. In German mythology, Frau Holle who is also known as Mother Holle, Mother Hulda or Old Mother Frost has a connection to weaving.

In the Celtic world, Brigantia might also be considered as a weaver goddess as she looked after the sovereignty of Britain and its people.

Honeysuckle   Uillean   (Inner Search)

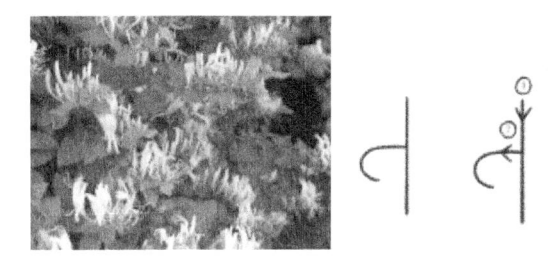

Uillean corresponds to the sound Ui, or Ua (sounding like Pe) in the Ogam alphabet and is associated with the Honeysuckle. This symbol represents manifesting of will, pathway to inner search and secrets.

Uillean pronounced: Pe

Element: Water, earth

Gender: Feminine

Powers: Uillean helps you to find hidden secrets.

Keywords

Path to inner search, hidden desires, secret wants, proceed with caution, goal of finding our true self.

Deities associated with Honeysuckle

Lugh, Muhn.

Tree Description

Most species of Honeysuckle are hardy twining climbers, but some species come as a shrub, most are deciduous, but some are evergreen. The leaves are opposite, and oval in shape, 1–10 cm long. Many of the species have sweetly scented, symmetrical tubular flowers that produce sweet, edible nectar, and mostly borne in clusters of two. The fruit is a red, blue or black spherical or elongated berries, that contain several seeds; in most species the berries are mildly poisonous, but in a few they are edible and grown for home use and commerce. Most honeysuckle berries are attractive to wildlife.

Uses

Honeysuckle can be brewed as a tea or used as incense. It is used mainly as a garden climbing shrub as it is sweet smelling. Nectar from the flowers can be enjoyed as a sweet treat. Both shrubby and vining sorts of honeysuckle have strong fibrous stems used in binding and textiles.

Interesting Spiritual Information

Honeysuckle shows you the way to help you help yourself by going on an inner search. It will present you with your hidden desires, secrets and the right path to help you search for yourself. But proceed with caution, for as you pursue your desires and experience pleasures, your hidden secrets are not necessarily impenetrable, but merely muted by background noise. It's up to you to work out what is true and what is not.

Tree Medicine

Honeysuckle is used for digestive disorders including pain and swelling (inflammation) of the small intestine (enteritis) and dysentery; upper respiratory tract infections including colds, influenza, swine flu, and pneumonia; other viral and bacterial infections; swelling of the brain (encephalitis); fever; boils; and sores. Honeysuckle is also used for urinary disorders, headache, diabetes, rheumatoid arthritis, and cancer. Some people use it to promote sweating, as a laxative, to counteract poisoning, and for birth control.

Honeysuckle is sometimes applied to the skin for inflammation and itching, and to kill germs.

Culpeper stated that only the leaves of the honeysuckle were used medicinally to treat coughs, sore throats and for opening obstructions of the liver and spleen. Gerard said that the flowers of the honeysuckle steeped in oil are good to help warm and soothe the body that is very cold.

Matthew Robinson in his New Family Herbal, shared Culpeper's view that honeysuckle leaves helped the spleen and liver. Matthew also recommended that the honeysuckle flowers are boiled in water and used as a poultice with a little oil added as a cure for hard swellings and abscesses.

Both the leaves and flowers of the honeysuckle are rich in salicylic acid, so may be used to relieve headaches, colds, flu, fever, aches, pains, arthritis and rheumatism. The leaves also have anti-inflammatory properties and contain antibiotics active against staphylococci and coli bacilli. Honeysuckle flowers and flower buds are used in various infusions and tinctures to treat coughs, catarrh, asthma, headaches and food poisoning.

Please note that honeysuckle berries are highly toxic and should NEVER be used on any account.

Herbal Medicine: Lonicera Caprifolium

Common Names: Woodbine

Parts Used: Flower

Overview: This is for the wild growing version rather than the ornamental variety. The flowers have an antimicrobial effect against salmonella, staphyloccus and streptococcus. In China, the herbalists there have used honeysuckle as an antibiotic herb for colds, flu and fevers. It has also been used for treating sore throats, conjunctivitis, and inflammations of the bowel, urinary tract and reproductive organs. It has been said that it is useful in treating cancer.

To get the best effect of the flowers, mix with the seeds of Forsythia suspensii (the yellow honeysuckle shrub), or Echinacea augustifolia or E. purpurea for a maximum antiviral and antibacterial effect.

Steep 2 teaspoons per cup for 20 mins. Drink a quarter of a cup x4 times a day.

Cautions: None found.

Ogam Channel Healing Guide

Spiritual/Mind: Anything traumatic   Affection   Coming into the present   Finding our true self   Free your heart's desire   Good luck   Hidden desires   Higher Self   Homesickness   Learn from the past without having to relive it   Inner freedom   Inner searching   Life threatening   Loving oneself   Psychic Vision   Nostalgia (loss of youth, health, beauty, significant emotional relationship) Tune into the unconditional love of Divinity   Secret wants   Self-worth   Soul freedom

Head/Neck: Eyes/ conjunctivitis   Headaches   Immune system   Sore throats   Swelling of the brain

Chest: Amygdalitis   Asthma   Cataplasm   Catarrh   Cleans the lungs/ viral and bacterial infections (tuberculosis, salmonella) Influenza   Swine flu   Depurative   Diabetes   Fever   Pnuemonia

Stomach: Diuretic   Digestive disorders   Expectorant, gentle laxative   Salmonella   Staphyloccus   Streptococcus

Liver: Liver Spleen

Urinary: Bladder   Urinary tract

Bowels: Inflammations of the bowel

Reproductive Organs: Inflammations of the reproductive organs

Skin: Boils/sores/ abscesses   Skin/ sun burns

Joints: Rheumatoid

Cancer: Cancer

General: Diabetes

Flower Remedy

Honeysuckle helps people who are living in the past instead of the present. People who dwell on their past happiness's (or past misfortunes) because they feel that their best days are behind them and that there is little or nothing to look forward to. Homesickness and nostalgia also link in with this state. The honeysuckle flower remedy helps one to access the past, learn from it without feeling the need to relive it. Then one can move forward into the present and enjoy today and tomorrow.

Notes

Other names for the honeysuckle include Irish vine, woodbine, fairy trumpets, honeybind, trumpet flowers, goat's leaf and sweet suckle. The old name, Woodbine, describes the twisting, binding nature of the honeysuckle through the hedgerows. There are variations on which forfeda characters refer to the honeysuckle. Some says it's the spiral, others, the cross hatch.

Folklore

In Scotland, village witches it is said, used honeysuckle in magical healing rituals by passing sick people through a wreath of honeysuckle 9 times. Then they would cut the plant into 9 pieces and burn it. There was also a belief that growing honeysuckle brought you good luck and would protect your home from evil.

Victorian suitors gave honeysuckle flowers as a promise of true love. Honeysuckle is said to attract friends, bring good luck, and sustain love in the home where it grows. When you bring its flowers into your home, they represent prosperity, and money is on its way.

Honeysuckle is very much liked by the fairies, and if you wish to have their presence in your home, it is essential to have some with you inside. Like the Fey themselves, honeysuckle thrives in liminal spaces, preferring fences and half-shade. A good tip: if you eat the blossoms from a honeysuckle bush, leave a few for the Fey.

Honeysuckle has folkloric associations with psychic vision and dreaming. Be careful if you leave open a garden window at night, because love dreams can travel on honeysuckle-scented air. When used in spells of gain, it is said to add a touch of sweetness to their energy. A honeysuckle plant growing outside the house is said to keep love alive and bring good fortune. Honeysuckle scent rubbed on faery offerings will make them too tasty to resist. There was a belief that if honeysuckle grew round the entrance to a home it actually prevented a witch from entering. If it grows well in your garden, then you will be protected from evil.

In Ireland, honeysuckle was used as a power against evil spirits and was used in a drink to cure the effects of the evil eye. When you brought its flowers into the house it will attract money.

The honeysuckle is a symbol of fidelity and affection. If you wear the flower it is said that you are able to dream of your true love. Its clinging nature symbolises that 'we are united in love,' and so emphasises the bond of devotion and affection between two people.

If the blooms were brought into the house, it is said that a wedding would follow within a year. But in the Victorian times, young girls were banned from bringing honeysuckle into the home because its heady fragrance was believed to cause risqué dreams.

Its wood has been used to make walking sticks because of its nature to grow around and entwine saplings. Its dried flowers are used for adding to pot-pourri, herb pillows and floral waters. Also, scented cosmetics are made from the fresh flowers.

Gooseberry   Iphin   (Spirit flowing)

Ogam letter IA or IO in the Ogam alphabet and is associated with the Gooseberry. This symbol represents the living Spirit flowing universally.

Iphin pronounced: IH-feen

Powers: Living Spirit universally flowing.

Keywords

New opportunities, power objects, women's cycles.

Deities associated with Gooseberry

Venus, Brigid, Arianrhod.

Tree Description

Gooseberry is native to Europe, the Caucasus and northern

Africa. The species has been naturalized in North America. The Gooseberry bush produces edible fruit on both a commercial and domestic basis. In the UK some sources say it is native, others say it has been introduced.

It is a straggling shrub which grows to about 1.5 m in height and width. Its stems become woody with a large thorn at each axil. The branches are thickly set with sharp spines, standing out singly or in groups of two or three from the bases of the short lateral leaf shoots.

The bell-shaped flowers with reddish leaves and smaller white-yellow petals on the bell's edge are produced, singly or in pairs. The deeply toothed leaves come in groups of 3 or 5 and are glossy, dark green. The fruit are berries, are generally hairy, usually green in colour, but sometimes red to purple, also have yellow, or white variants. The egg-shaped berry contains many seeds in its center and can be as large as 1inch long.

Uses

Gooseberries are edible raw, or used as an ingredient in desserts, such as pies, tarts, fools and crumbles. The early pickings tend to be generally sour and more appropriate for culinary use. They can be used to flavour soft drinks, water and milk and made into fruit wines and teas. They are preserved in jams, as dried fruit, used in pickling, or stored in sugar syrup.

Interesting Spiritual Information

It is seen as the sweetest of wood/life, has a wonderful taste, has divine influences which surround us in the sweetest ways, with kindred spirits of nature.

Tree Medicine

It is said to be good for digestive complaints, fever and the monthly period. Gooseberries can be quite beneficial to the heart and lower cholesterol levels, ultimately reducing the risk of heart disease. Powerful antioxidants are also suggested to support heart health. Respiratory disorders including tuberculosis of the lungs, asthma, chronic cough, cold and bronchitis. It reduces the blood sugar in diabetes. Tones up the functions of all the organs and renews body energy. Good for eyesight, conjunctivitis and glaucoma.

Also helps with rheumatism and scurvy. It improves body resistance and protects against infection. It is an accepted hair tonic in traditional recipes for enriching hair growth and hair pigmentation. The berries are an excellent source of vitamin C. It also helps purify the blood.

The juice was said to cure all inflammations. Gooseberry consists of a huge variety of minerals and vitamins useful in treating menstrual cramps. Regular consumption of Gooseberry juice along with honey is beneficial for eyesight. Gooseberry also helps the body absorb calcium in a positive way.

Ogam Channel Healing Guide

Spiritual/Mind: Access your inner wisdom   Engage in new opportunities   Good for psychological stress during menopause   Guilt and incompleteness with the inability to have children or nurture them   Inner Guidance   Lacking Confidence   Low self-esteem   Mental uncertainty   Turns fear into engagement with life   Tuning to your inner knowing   Working with power objects

Head/Neck: Ageing Maintaining strength   Body resistance   Infection   Eyesight   Conjunctivitis   Glaucoma   Hair growth and colour   Intra ocular tension   Improves body resistance and protects against infection

Chest: Diabetes   Fever   Heart Disease   Lower cholesterol   Reduces blood sugars in diabetes   Respiratory disorders including tuberculosis of the lungs, asthma, chronic cough, cold and bronchitis

Stomach: Digestive complaints

Skin: Scurvy

Reproductive: Monthly period

Joints: Rheumatism.

Organs: Tones up all organs and boosts body energy

General: Renews body energy.

Flower Remedy

Gooseberry is used when you are not trusting your own deeper knowing and are looking outside of yourself for answers. When you are not recognizing yourself as a wise soul with a deep well of wisdom. If you are having difficulty adjusting to sudden changes or to new opportunities in life. Specific symptoms can include emotional outbursts, mental uncertainty, not able to sense inner guidance.

Black Gooseberry encourages you to turn to your inner knowing. It supports you and the inner wisdom you have to draw upon. As you become better aligned within, it means you can access your wisdom, and use it to deal with sudden changes in your life.

Notes

There is not much information to be found on the noble gooseberry, apart from recipe books. There are no obvious ties to myths, legends or much to be found in folklore. What there is I have included below. An elusive little number but with much to give as in food and in healing.

Folklore

Gooseberry has traditionally been used in childbirth and for menstrual problems. For this reason, gooseberry was considered sacred to the goddesses Brighid and Arianrhod who oversaw matters of childbirth and women's cycles.

In the 19th-century, Gooseberry bush was slang for pubic hair, and from this comes the saying that babies are *born under a gooseberry bush*.

Playing gooseberry is an English saying aimed at an unwanted extra person, like a chaperone, when young lovers are in each other's company.

The phrase *great gooseberry season* is used by newspapers to describe a period where there isn't much headline news so tales like the largest gooseberry in history are published instead.

The phrase *going gooseberrying* involves stealing clothes that are hanging out on lines to dry.

There is a strong association with faeries.

Beech   Eamhancholl   (Insight)

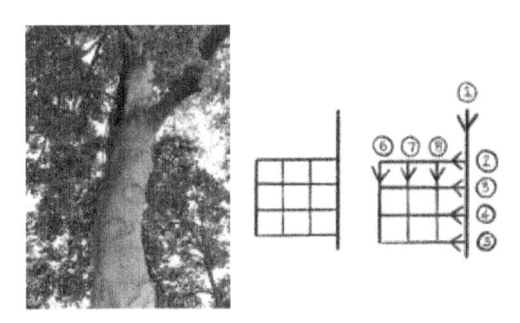

Eamhancholl corresponds to the letter AE ans X in the Ogam alphabet and is associated with the Beech tree. This symbol represents ancient knowledge, insight and learning.

Pronounced: EH-mun kuhl

Element: Air, Earth

Powers: Ancient knowledge revealed.

Keywords

Ancient knowledge, old objects, places and writing, guidance, insight, protection, solid foundations, learning, wishes, freedom from fixed ideas.

Deities associated with Beech

Saturn, Chronos, Old Father time, Ogma, Hermes/Mercury, Odin, Fagus, Ceridwen.

Tree Description

Beech is a deciduous tree native to temperate Europe, Asia, and North America. It can grow to the towering heights of 30-40m with an enormous and spreading crown. The bark is smooth and light grey, often covered in a green algae. The leaves are either entirely or sparsely toothed, from 5–15 cm long and 4–10 cm broad. Beeches are monoecious, bearing both male and female flowers on the same plant. The small flowers are unisexual, the female flowers borne in pairs, the male flowers wind-pollinating catkins. They arrive in spring quickly after the new leaves appear.

The fruit is a small, sharply three–angled nut 10–15 mm long, either single or in pairs in soft-spined husks 1.5–2.5 cm long, known as cupules. Its nuts are edible, but are bitter due to high tannin content, and are called beechnuts or beechmast.

Uses

Beech wood is used in the making of drums, handles for tools and stocks on military weapons. Its wood chips are used to smoke sausages or other meats and to dry out malt for beers. Beer manufacturers use beech as a *fining* agent in the brewing process to help enhance the flavor. Beech-nuts are used to fatten pigs. Artists used beech soot mixed with water to make a transparent ink/pigment called "soot brown", or bistre.

Beech wood is an excellent firewood, easily split and burns for a long time calmly. The textile modal is a rayon often made wholly from reconstituted cellulose of pulped beech wood. It is also used in furniture framing, flooring, engineering purposes, in plywood and in household items like plates, but rarely as a decorative wood. The timber can be used to build chalets, houses, and log cabins.

Nuts are pressed for edible oil. Beech leaves in spring are used as a fine salad vegetable, as sweet as a mild cabbage, though much softer in texture. Young leaves steeped in gin for several weeks and sweetened to give a liqueur called beech leaf novau.

The bark was used by Indo-European people for writing-related purposes, especially in religious context. Beech wood tablets were a common writing material in Germanic societies before the development of paper. A semi-drying oil comes from the seed and is used as a fuel for lighting and a lubricant for polishing wood. The seed residue is poisonous.

Leaf buds harvested in the winter and dried on the twigs are used as toothpicks. Leaves gathered in autumn are used as a stuffing material for mattresses. The wood has often been used as a source of creosote, tar, methyl alcohol and acetic acid.

Interesting Spiritual Information

Long ago, beech tablets were used to write upon. Both beech and book come from the same word origins. Beech is associated with ancient knowledge as revealed in old objects, places and writing. It can indicate guidance from the past to gain an insight which protects and provides a solid base upon which to rely on. Beech is sometimes thought of as the Mother of the wood, or Beech Queen, consort to the Oak King. The beech is well known for her generosity of spirit as she gives both protection and nourishment, her branches fan outwards into a broad canopy (and seen as the source of inspiration to those who designed and built the early cathedrals) for shelter and her nuts as a valuable food source. Beech was also used as a good luck charm.

Tree Medicine

The bark is antacid, antipyretic, antiseptic, antitussive, expectorant and odontalgic. A tar (or creosote) is obtained through dry distillation of the branches and is used internally as a stimulating expectorant and externally as an antiseptic to various skin diseases or wounds. It has the potential to aid in providing relief from eczema, psoriasis, boils, frostbite and burns. Pure creosote has been used in giving relief from toothache but should never be used without expert guidance.

Bark preparation was used to help reduce fever. The bark is rich in lignans and other antioxidant substances that can be a major boost to your immune system. Antioxidants can neutralize free radicals which cause chronic disease and cell mutation, including cancer. By drying the bark and treating it properly, it becomes a viable source of highly beneficial antioxidant compounds.

Beech tree leaves and shoots have been eaten for hundreds of years, particularly in times of famine. The high cellulose and fibre content are extremely good for regulating digestion. The leaves can also be boiled down to create a poultice or a salve with proven analgesic properties. These can reduce headaches and other pain related issues. It works for both topical application and oral consumption. A poultice made from the leaves helped to heal scabs and water collected from the hollows of ancient beeches was thought to heal many skin complaints. Stuffing your mattress with beech leaves was acknowledged as a way of speeding up the healing process.

Beechnuts have been used for food for both humans and animals for many years. The high levels of vitamin B6 in the nuts make it a great addition for pregnant mothers and their babies. It is also known as folate or folic acid, an essential vitamin in preventing neural tube defects in infants.

Although the seeds are considered toxic when used in large quantities, a decoction can be made to boost kidney function and stimulate urination. As a diuretic, beech can clear toxins from out the body, including excess fats, salts, waste and water, so improving your metabolism efficiency.

Herbal Medicine: Fagus sylvatica

Common Name: Beech.

Parts Used: Nut oil, tar from the wood.

Overview: The traditional use of the oil and tar for chest and skin diseases has now decreased to the point where it is not much used in modern medicine.

Phytochemicals:

Oil: Fixed oil.

Tar: Distilled beech tar yields creosote.

Actions: The tar is believed to be antiseptic and expectorant.

Indications:

Internally: Chronic bronchitis, skin diseases (including psoriasis), wet coughs.

Preparations

Internally: Bach flower remedy.

Externally: The oil and tar are not readily available.

Cautions: Beech has largely fallen out of use and should only be used on expert professional advice.

Ogam Channel Healing Guide

Spiritual/Mind: Access to ancient knowledge   Arrogance   Meet your inner guide   Criticism   Fault finding   For mental clarity   Freedom from fixed ideas   Guidance   Insight

Intolerance   Judgement on others   Lack sympathy   Learning Mental-health issue as in depression, fear, anxiety and self-worth issues   Opening up to inner and outer beauty   Personal development   Pride   Protection   Solid   Symbolism   Truth Wishes   Writing

Head/Neck: Headache   Immune system   Toothache

Stomach: Digestion   Worms

Kidney: Clears toxins from the body, including excess fats, salt, waste, and water. Stimulates urination

Skin: Skin diseases; eczema, psoriasis, boils, frostbite and burns

General: Metabolic system

Flower Remedy

Beech remedy is for people who feel the need to see better and beauty in their lives. People who are in a *beech-state* tend to have outbursts of irritability, lacking the compassion and understanding that other people have different routes towards perfection. As a vibrational essence, beech is used against mental rigidity, fault finding, intolerance, arrogance, criticism, pride, lack of sympathy and judgement of others. It helps us let go of fixed ideas and opinions that limit our progress through life and also our personal development.

Notes

Beeches were called 'Boc' by the Anglo-Saxons, the word later became book. Today the Swedish word 'Bok' means both book and beech, in German, 'Buch' means book and 'Buche' means beech. When material words were inscribed, they took on the power and magic of the gods. It is why the beech tree was held in such awe as it allowed wisdom to be passed on to future generations.

Folklore

Beech is associated with femininity and is often considered the queen of British trees, where oak is the king. In Celtic mythology, Fagus was the god of beech trees. Beech groves have been found in or close to important places of power.

Many legends talk of serpents and beech trees and the poet Tennyson referred to the *serpent-rooted Beech tree*. In Britain it is often associated with snakes and earth energies due to its serpentine root system, thus leading the beech to having Underworld connections.

In the medieval Welsh poem, The Battle of the Trees, by the bard Taliesin, it refers to the beech tree which prospers through spells and litanies. Thus, showing its close ties to magic and magical lore.

The goddess Ceridwen as Henwen, the great ancient white sow, possessed great wisdom from eating nuts from beneath the sacred Beech tree. Helen of Troy apparently carved her lover's name upon a beech tree. Jason built the Argo with beech in preference to oak.

The Irish god Ogma, a leading warrior of the Tuatha de Danaan, who was credited with the writing of the Ogam Alphabet, wrote upon Beech.

Beech is linked with time, wisdom and knowledge but especially written wisdom, as it was used in thin slices to write upon and form the very first books.

15

Preparing to give Ogam Healing

It is important for the Ogam practitioner to be as stress free as possible before undertaking a healing session for another person, or indeed themselves. This can easily be attained by the following methods:

Controlling your breathing, relaxing the body and creating a peaceful state of mind.

By taking three deep and controlled breaths your body will physically start to relax, any stress levels will begin to calm themselves and your mind can focus in on what you are about to do. You might also like to ask your client to do the same thing to help themselves relax too.

An Ogam healing session can last between 30 minutes to an hour, it is really up to both yourself and the client. It is during this time that you will be channelling healing Ogam energy from the inner world through your own and into your client's body to the area that needs healing. As you develop your practise of Ogam healing, you will find yourself developing your own approach in terms of time and location of each hand position, based on your own intuition.

When a client comes with a joint problem, it is obvious to concentrate on that area and any other that has come to you when you diagnosed the body at the beginning of the session. You can never give too much or too little with Ogam as it is divine in nature and therefore will work for the highest good of both the giver and receiver.

Ogam Self-Healing

The hand positions for self-healing are in most cases identical to those used when treating others. It is very important that the Ogam practitioner gives him/herself Ogam as regularly as possible. After a few treatments you will be able to feel beneficial effects on your physical, emotional and mental health. You will be able to deal with issues in your life much easier. To give a self-healing either lie or sit comfortably and put your hands in the hand positions as outlined earlier in this book.

Create your personal grove and call in the elements/dragons, visualize the intended Ogam tree and its symbol. Chant its name three times and draw the symbol in front of you. See and feel the energy being channelled through your crown chakra into your heart and place your hands at position 1. Then intend the Ogam energy to flow. See/feel it channel from your heart out your hands and into your client. Hold each position for at least 3-5 minutes, then move your hands slowly to the next position.

Ogam can be given at regular times of the day as part of your own meditation or healing routine. If you can't commit to a specific time, try when you have spare time.

An option to this way of working is to open up your grove and journey to the tree you wish to use and sit within the healing energy and see /feel it working on the area you wish to heal within.

A Spiritual Process

Giving and receiving Ogam can sometimes be a profoundly enriching experience for all concerned. It is not unusual for you, if you are sensitive, to pick up some psychic information from or about your client during the treatment. You can always ask for this information too by having specific questions ready.

This occurs due to the interaction of the energy fields between you and the client and often leads to a greater awareness of your client's condition. Whether you choose to divulge this extra information is up to you. Please use your common sense. If you think it may be helpful, then do so. But never divulge what you have uncovered to a third party. Remember the privacy and confidentiality of your client comes first.

Body Positions on a Chair or Healing Couch/Settee

Self-healing is normally done lying down, but we are all different and some healers and clients will have their own reasons to choose whether it be on a chair, healing couch or settee.

Healing on a Chair

Make sure the client is sitting comfortably with their arms and legs uncrossed and feet flat on the ground. This will help the energy to flow unimpeded and help to create an automatic positive grounding effect. If their feet are too short to touch the ground, place a cushion under them, or behind their back. Their hands can be placed on either leg, close to the body.

Their base of spine should be placed against the back of the chair as this keeps their back upright and the head and neck are more likely to be in line with the spine to help with the positive flow of energy. If possible, ask them to close their eyes so that they may passively experience the biofeedback (see below) instead of looking round the room or checking you out and so perhaps blocking the energy flow through negative or questioning thoughts.

Healing on Couch/Settee

By using a healing couch, it can be perceived as the professional way for this type of therapy and treatment. Try to use paper towel (couch paper) on the pillow as a sign of cleanliness and along the length of the couch. Remember to give them gentle assistance on and off the couch. Their limbs should be uncrossed, and eyes closed for the same reasons as above. Provide a blanket or sheet as their bodies will drop a few degrees in heat due to inactivity, and they might get cold if they fall asleep. They might of course politely refuse and that is ok too.

Ogam Treatment Checklist

- Before the client arrives cleanse yourself, the room, chair or couch by smudging with sage, or with Ogam energy.

- Be relaxed and at one with yourself, don't rush around.

- Have a box of tissues to hand, just in case.

- Have a jug of water with two glasses.

- Keep your toilet/bathroom facilities clean and hygienic.

- Spend a few minutes with the client, gain a rapport and check they have enough time for you to complete the treatment.

- Explain the Ogam process and hand positions.

- Answer any questions the client may have.

- Ensure interruptions will not occur, switch off phone and secure door if appropriate.

- If you are to play music, set at low volume, get CD player to repeat. Also don't forget to ask the client whether they want to listen to music. Some don't.

- Make sure you are both comfortable and that you can retain a relaxed posture during the entire treatment. Ask the client to take 3 deep breaths before you start.

- You can create your healing grove, acknowledge your guardian, bring in the elements and then tune into the specific tree energy you wish to use. Draw your symbol over their body, OR just draw the symbol above the client's body and bring in the energy you have been attuned to. Then begin treatment using techniques and hand positions taught.

- Remember, once you have finished the front of the body, you don't have to turn the client over for the back, as you can work through the body to reach it!

- After completing treatment, spend a few minutes thanking your Ogam spirits/deities for their assistance in the process.

- Ask the client to take 3 deep breaths and to "come back into the room in their own time." If asleep, apply *slight* pressure on feet, shoulders or back, until they come back to full consciousness.

- If they request water, give it to them.

- Take time to talk through treatment, indicating any feelings gained or advice for further treatments.

- Ensure the client has your details and can contact you for further advice or assistance.

- Keep a record of your client and their details, eg name, address, phone etc

- You might also wish to write up what happened during the session for your own records.

- Relax

16

Biofeedback Sensations Explained

Biofeedback sensations are what you as a practitioner or the client might experience during the course of working with Ogam tree healing energy. You might experience some, all, or none of these sensations, but as and when you do, be aware they are natural phenomenon and are there to guide you.

Touch (Or Feeling)

Heat, cold, and electrical tingling are the most common biofeedback experience of the sense of touch/feeling. All biofeedback sensations vary from very slight up to extremely intense.

Heat can be gentle warmth, or a severe burning sensation.

Cold can be a little coolness, or as freezing as a block of ice. Cold energy is needed for some conditions such as bones, tumours, and bacterial infection.

Electrical tingling

The electrical sensation can be like slight pins and needles, or like a giant electric shock. The shock re-energizes a depleted biosystem.

Vibration/shaking

Vibration can happen while a client is adjusting to the energy frequency. Shaking may also happen to some people who practise meditation, yoga, or prayer. If Ogam energy comes up against an energy block, there may be vibration as that block is pushed against and eventually cleared.

Pushing or pulling

This is the magnetic nature of the energy at work. Pushing is usually due to the positive and intelligent nature of Ogam energy pushing into negative energy to disperse it. Pulling is usually due to the positive and intelligent Ogam energy pulling away, often taking negative energy from the body.

Circular or spiralling motion

It could be due to the natural spiralling nature of energy as it flows from above into or out of your being – rather like water spiralling down a sink.

Feeling as if falling over

This can be either an etheric or a physical issue. Etheric falling over is when it seems as if you are falling to one side. Occasionally this falling feeling is so much that you may even put one leg out to stop yourself falling. But when you look, you notice that you did not move. This is the Etheric body being re-balanced.

Movement of energy outside the body

A gentle breeze, or a huge wind. Energy is moving around the body.

Movement of energy inside the body

This can mean various things. The twitch of a muscle denotes an energising of that area. Rippling of muscles, e.g. up and down a leg, does not happen often, but is interesting to watch. It represents muscle revitalisation. A rod of energy building up inside is a reconnection to get something going again.

Light-headed / dizzy/ sick

This is relatively common, and you may need to explain it to your client to prevent unnecessary worry. This is a progression where someone may first feel light-headed. If Ogam energy gets stronger, the feeling progresses to dizziness. Then, if Ogam is extremely intense, sickness.

Loss of Energy

Ogam can take away stressed energy and replace it with positive energy. The body's stressed electrical energy can also be grounded or earthed during healing, leaving the feeling that energy has been taken away. Either way, there will be enough of the client's natural energy body left to build on, so that they will be able to return to a normal way of life.

Pain

During Ogam healing, pain may occur for various reasons, but is usually a sign of excellent healing. The main issue will be to reassure your client that the pain is there for a positive reason!

Seeing Through Physical Eyes

The biofeedback potentials are nearly the same for both physical and third eye. The difference being that vision from the third eye can be achieved with the normal eyes closed.

Psychic Vision Sight – Through Third Eye

As stated above, the biofeedback of sight and vision can be from the two normal eyes, or the third eye.

Colours

The physical and psychic visions of colour are common and important because during an Ogam treatment or when tuning into

Ogam energy through the chakras it is normal for the more clairvoyant-type people to see colours.

The past in this life or a previous life

If a past life arises in a vision it is not to be explored, unless you are qualified in counselling, psychotherapy, hypnotherapy etc. If you wish to explore past lives connected with this one, only do so if you know what you are doing and with client consent.

Psychic visions

There are many possible psychic visions. Most are relevant to a reality that the person is just starting to discover. Discuss with your client and remember that spirit speaks in metaphor, symbols as well as through direct revelation. You might also want to vet what you have been given as nobody likes bad news given blandly. Be empathetic!

Guides

Ogam healing allies may well make themselves known to the practitioner during healing. You may also see them working on the client. You may well see your guardian of the grove, tree spirits, deities and other allies that wish to work with you.

Hearing

During an Ogam treatment, sounds may be heard, or thoughts appear from your own higher consciousness, guardian, tree spirits, deities and allies.

Smell

Smelling energy is like hearing energy. Some spirits have their signature smells. A high being such as a deity or teacher may smell of frankincense, roses or beech wood. A dead friend or relative may come in with a smell you would know them for if you thought about it, such as soup if they were known for cooking a type of soup, or a particular brand of tobacco or perfume.

Taste

As above. But it is relatively rare to taste illnesses, guides, etc. When working and extracting negative energy, I often get a feeling of repulsion in my stomach and gag (not too loudly as this might worry the patient).

Spiritual Biofeedback

Spiritual biofeedback can come in many ways, such as seeing or experiencing a deity being: There are many deities working with the Ogam energies, check with the list for each tree. There might of course be new ones wishing to make themselves known.

Angels may also appear. If you know the name of the angel, don't be scared, they are there for a positive reason, so talk with them. Ask them why they are present and for why. Some people who have developed spiritually may even have the beautiful and deeply emotional experience of themselves as an angel.

Seeing a white light. If you see a spiritual white light, it will be the brightest light you could imagine.

Uncontrollable laughter may come when you are connecting into the ecstasy of deity nature. Occasionally giggling or laughter is because the client inwardly understands that a most profound healing has occurred.

Ecstasy is when a client is experiencing a feeling like all the most positive emotions you could ever have, happening at the same time.

17

Case Studies

The following case studies comes from several direct and distant healings I undertook in the research phase of this study. There are also a few examples of people using the training on themselves or on others.

"I had asked Thomas to understand, connect and communicate with spirit better and to find my own unique way to do this. Since having the sessions, I feel my connection to spirit is very much stronger in so many ways, feelings, visions and impressions seem so much clearer and my intuition has suddenly increased." - CG Cambridge.

"I had 3 healings with Thomas. Immune system, anxiety and stress, and bruising/swelling with added elements. I had distance healing and what can I say? I feel changed in a few areas of my life for the better. The change was instant after each healing. I feel I am more in the now meaning I stress less. I am very well in terms of health, to the point people are telling me they have never known me to be this well physically. Also, to top it off my psychic/intuition has definitely become stronger since having the healing. Each healing gave me different sensations and were programmed to a time that suited me. What has impressed me the most is how much my bruising from an injury has gone down. It had been there for weeks and the morning after my healing it was pretty much next to nothing. I can't thank Thomas enough for the strength and power he has helped me tap into." -SH Cambridge

NH: She has Polymyalgia pain in her neck and legs and at times her joints lock in her jaw and fingers:

First healing: "Just wanted to update you! My mum actually fell asleep 10 mins into her (distant healing) treatment and the great thing is she has a sleeping problem! The next day she was able to be a lot more productive. Usually, the pain stops her doing things and her mind was a lot clearer. Whereas before she only focuses on the negatives and ends up not doing anything. She seems much brighter to me as well!"

Second healing: "Just to let you know my mum is doing much better. She hasn't spent a day in bed since last healing. She is in much better spirits and is working on her mental health now that her body is stronger. It's great to see her so bubbly again, she is very spritely, and I am happy to see it! She said the shift she has felt since the healing is very strong. She doesn't ever use her pain relief wheat bag as she doesn't need it anymore." - NH Cambridge

"I wanted to say a massive thank you for this spiritual healing. It was a great experience and I'm really appreciative. I found the whole experience very revitalizing. I felt like a big weight came off my shoulders after your healing and I don't feel burdened by an overload of emotion any longer. I feel like your healing contributed to a really positive attitude shift in myself, and I can only say that things have been going my way since then." -VH Cambridge

Self-Healing

"My back was a bit sore today & I used the Silver Birch symbol on myself when I had a massage this evening…It seemed to have a relaxing elongation effect on my spine. It felt a lot easier after. - SR London

Practitioner Healing

"I have used the trees and dragons with several clients either during sessions or separately, with powerful results. I also had a go with Blackthorn…wow…heavy going for a heavy case! Was told to follow up with Silver Birch the next day and that went well too!" - NA London

Feedback Forms

1)   JK Cambridge

How Did You Feel Before the Healing Session?

Bad experience on holiday where a boy attempted to rape me. Since then, I have suffered terrible self-worth, great anxiousness and unable to have sex with my boyfriend.

How Did You Feel During the Session?

Safe and secure.

How Did You Feel After the Sessions?

Very peaceful, in charge of my own feelings and very grounded.

Did You Have Any Unique Experiences?

I had a vision of walking naked in the woods, happy and free and then by a lake with lots of naked men where we all got along greatly, bathing and having fun. I was aware of Blackthorn energy and my Power animal (Lion) being beside me.

2)   CG Cambridge

How Did You Feel Before the Healing Session?

I wanted help tuning into my spiritual side. I tried to relax myself by using my deep breathing technique as it had been a very busy day at work - I was a bit wound up.

How Did You Feel During the Session?

I could feel myself getting warm and had tingles in my arms, started to feel very relaxed.

How Did You Feel After the Sessions?

It was really more a few hours later that I started to feel anything. It felt like my body was vibrating, this has lasted a few days now, especially when I lay down in bed, I can really feel it. I have felt tingling in my third eye area ever since too, more noticeable at night when I'm laying down.

Did You Have Any Unique Experiences?

All of the above and more ☺ I have been seeing images through third eye all the time and having colour pictures of people shown to me, I just shut my eyes and they are there. I can hear voices too periodically; I only just manage to pick up what they are saying then they go. I constantly see colours and swirls patterns.

Any Other Comments?

I feel this session was so beneficial, I feel like I have finally moved forward in my spiritual awakening in leaps and bounds.... Thank you, Tom.

3)   TI Cambridge

How Did You Feel Before the Healing Session?

Tense, stressed, short fused and fed up

How Did You Feel During the Session?

Relaxed, clear minded, sleepy but alert.

How Did You Feel After the Sessions?

Very chilled, connected and in tune. Like I could feel nice energy flowing through my veins.

Did You Have Any Unique Experiences?

Yes, I had a lot of visions and dreams about gardening, roots, plants and garden gnomes, haha! I also woke up and found myself running my fingers across the top of each hand, I had been doing it in my sleep. I was once told by a reflexologist to do this to help strengthen immune system, so it was interesting to know I was doing this in my sleep! I also woke up very thirsty and still am so drinking lots of water today! More relaxed and less stressed.

Any Other Comments?

Thank you!

4) FD Cambridge

How Did You Feel Before the Healing Session?

A little anxious about an event I had the next day.

How Did You Feel During the Session?

Quite neutral. In the now! Chilled but not overly sleepy.

How Did You Feel After the Sessions?

Clear minded, like I had space for thought and less clutter

Did You Have Any Unique Experiences?

I had visions as I was dozing about blue lights, like electricity moving around as if it was going around circuits.

Any Other Comments?

I was very relaxed on the way to and during event. I also didn't drink at the event and felt confident in my own skin! I am more "in the now" rather than thinking of past or worrying about the future.

5) CB Cambridge

How Did You Feel Before the Healing Session?

I did a breathing meditation for about 15 mins before the time of our agreed session (7:30pm), so I felt quite relaxed. Although I did have slightly anxious feeling in my stomach (I get this a lot)

How Did You Feel During the Session?

About 10 minutes into the session, I started to feel quite warm and a lot more relaxed. I could feel mild tingles through body.

How Did You Feel After the Sessions?

Immediately after I felt very light, like a weight had been lifted from me, the anxious feeling in stomach had gone.

Did You Have Any Unique Experiences?

I was imagining sitting under a huge oak tree on the grass and leaning back on the tree, I seemed to be able to really visualise this, the bark of the tree was especially memorable, I could see every grain, lump and bump.

About 20 minutes in I felt like pressure had been taken away from me (from my stomach and chest area), like a release of some sort. This was definitely a strong emptying feeling so to speak.

Any Other Comments?

I didn't know what to expect but was pleasantly surprised of how relaxing this was.

6) JM London

How Did You Feel Before the Healing Session?

Un-centred, anxious and out of kilter. Lots going on at work and getting married in two weeks' time.

How Did You Feel During the Session?

Safe and secure.

How Did You Feel After the Sessions?

Grounded, peaceful and happy.

Did You Have Any Unique Experiences?

As Ogam healing was taking place I felt that my body had become like bark of a great tree, very calming and peaceful.

7) WM London

How Did You Feel Before the Healing Session?

Suffering from Alzheimers

How Did You Feel During the Session?

Safe and secure.

How Did You Feel After the Sessions?

Very peaceful, much loved and very grounded.

Did You Have Any Unique Experiences?

I saw colours

Any Other Comments?

I feel good.

Thomas Marty Healing and Training

Healing

Ogam Tree Healing and Shamanic Healing via website

www.martyshamanichealing.com

Training

Ogam Tree Healing For Beginners Course available via website.

Shamanic Practitioner Training available via website.

Shamanic Counselling training available via website.

Divination Workshop available via website.

Working with the Elements Workshops via website.

Ancestral Web Healing Workshop available via website.

Spirit of the Wand Workshop available via website.

Wand Making Workshops available via website.

Bibliography

A Druid's Herbal for the Sacred Year by Ellen Evert Hopman

Celtic Tree Magic – Ogham Lore and Druid Mysteries by Danu Forest.

Cunningham's Encyclopaedia of Magical Herbs by Scott Cunningham

Druid Mysteries by Philip Carr-Gomm

Encyclopaedia of Magical Herbs by Scott Cunningham

Gossip from the Forest by Sara Maitland

Ogam, The Celtic Oracle of the Trees by Paul Rhys Mountfort

Shamanic Healing by Peter Aziz

The Book of Druidry by Ross Nichols

The Celtic Tree Oracle: A System of Divination by Liz and Colin Murray

The Celtic Wisdom of Trees Jane Gifford

The Druids by Stuart Piggott

The Ever-Changing woodlands by Readers Digest

The Healing Energies of Trees by Patrice Bouchardon

The Healing Power of Celtic Plants Angela Paine

The Hidden Life of Trees by Peter Wohileben

The Mammoth Book of Ancient Wisdom by Cassandra Eason

The Tarot Bible by Sarah Bartlett

The World Tree in Classical Shamanism by Karen Kelly 1996

Trees Collins gem all you need to know by Alastair Fitter and David More

Trees and How They Grow by G Clarke Nuttall

Tree Medicine Peter Conway

Tree Wisdom – the Definitive Guidebook to the Myth, Folklore and Healing Power of Trees by Jacqueline Memory Paterson

The White Goddess by Robert Graves

Birch Symbolism http://www.bartleby.com/101/378.html

Celtic Tree Magic by Danu Forest

Voice of the Trees by Mickie Mueller

Weaving Word Wisdom by Erynn Rowan Kaurie

Trees for Life http://treesforlife.org.uk/forest/birch/

The Woodland Trust https://www.woodlandtrust.org.uk

https://treesforlife.org.uk/forest/mythology-folklore Paul Kendall

http://www.icysedgwick.com/willow-folklore/

https://www.bachcentre.com/centre/remedies.htm

https://www.woodlandtrust.org.uk/visiting-woods/trees-woods-and-wildlife/british-trees/native-trees/

www.thegoddesstree.com

www.thriveonnews.com

www.livinglibraryblog.com

www.talesunfold.com

https://www.whitedragon.org.uk/articles/apple.htm

https://www.hunker.com/13428615/uses-for-apple-trees

http://www.flowermeaning.com/heather-flower-meaning/

http://www.naturalmedicinalherbs.net/herbs/e/euonymus-europaeus=spindle-tree.php

https://norse-mythology.net/yggdrasil-in-norse-mythology/

http://www.shamaniccircles.org/2002oraclefolder/worldtree.html

https://contemporaryshaman.wordpress.com/2016/03/19/the-shamans-tree-in-a-contemporary-world/

Flower remedies:

https://yorkshire-flower-essences.myshopify.com/products/metal-excess

http://www.ecoenchantments.co.uk/myogham_yewpage.html: Ogam trees and info

http://www.ecoenchantments.co.uk/myhomepage.html: Ogam info healing etc…

https://www.pharmaceutical-journal.com/opinion/blogs/anticancer-properties-of-silver-birch/

https://www.organicfacts.net/health-benefits/fruit/rowan-berries.html

https://en.heilkraeuter.net/herbs/rowan-berry.htm

https://thedaughterofthesun.wordpress.com/2015/09/01/rowan-treemedicinal-propertiesuses/

http://herbs-treatandtaste.blogspot.com/2011/02/ash-tree-health-benefits-uses-and.html

https://www.herbwisdom.com/herb-holly.html

https://www.botanical.com/botanical/mgmh/v/vine--09.html

http://www.bio.brandeis.edu/fieldbio/medicinal_plants/pages/Domestic_Grape.htm

https://www.organicfacts.net/health-benefits/other/ivy.html

https://www.herbal-supplement-resource.com/english-ivy-herbs.html

http://www.naturalmedicinalherbs.net/herbs/p/phragmites-australis=common-reed.php

https://www.pharmaceutical-journal.com/opinion/blogs/medicinal-properties-of-blackthorn/11084777.blog?firstPass=false

https://ayushology.com/health-benefits-of-herbs/health-benefits-of-sloe-berries/

https://www.incredible-edible-todmorden.co.uk/apothecary/the-elder-tree

https://www.herbazest.com/herbs/aspen

http://www.naturalmedicinalherbs.net/herbs/t/taxus-baccata=yew.php

http://www.naturalmedicinalherbs.net/herbs/e/euonymus-europaeus=spindle-tree.php

https://botanical.com/botanical/mgmh/s/spindl82.html

https://www.gyanunlimited.com/health/top-10-medicinal-and-health-benefits-of-amla-or-indian-gooseberry/11117/

https://www.organicfacts.net/health-benefits/other/beech.html